OFF THE MAP

OFF THE MAP

Bicycling Across Siberia

～～～～～

Mark Jenkins

WILLIAM MORROW AND COMPANY, INC.
New York

Library of Congress Cataloging-in-Publication Data

Jenkins, Mark (Mark D.)
    Off the map : bicycling across Siberia / Mark Jenkins.
        p.   cm.
    ISBN 0-688-09546-1
    1. Siberia (R.S.F.S.R.)—Description and travel—1981–
2. Jenkins, Mark (Mark G.)—Journeys—Russian S.F.S.R.—Siberia.
3. Bicycle touring—Russian S.F.S.R.—Siberia.   I. Title.
DK756.J46   1992
915.704′854—dc20   91-17310
                                                                              CIP

Printed in the United States of America

First Edition

1   2   3   4   5   6   7   8   9   10

BOOK DESIGN BY PAUL CHEVANNES

To Sue

Suffering is the origin of consciousness.
Fyodor Dostoyevsky

The bicycle is the noblest invention of mankind.
William Saroyan

*You cannot travel on the path before you
have become the Path itself.*
Gautama Buddha

PART ONE

I

IN A SLOUGH. Mud beneath the clearings. Mud beneath the pressing white birches thin and naked as humans.

Mud in my mouth but I keep riding. Standing out of the saddle dancing wumping spitting riding hard as I can because they catch you if you go slow. Rise from the swamp and light on your face and arms and grow thick and blacken your skin till it's burning. So I ride with my eyes mostly closed and teeth clinched and nose down drooling but my ears are lost, they carom inside screeching.

The path breaks from the trees. I am so far away and still riding. Breathing and riding, down the wicked trail through sinking wet grass. I know what is coming but I keep on, thighs churning, heat thickening around my chest. I am dropping. The sky arches off and mud pours in and I'm thrashing foundering dropping like a deer shot in a swamp.

Then I see the little girl yesterday. Couldn't have been yesterday, just flutters that close to the surface. Must be weeks ago by now, years.

This little girl she lives in a Russian mud village with a mud road going in and no road going out. There are log cabins with flowers in the windows.

Amazing she has a bicycle big as a horse. She can't reach the

saddle. Her crotch forks down on the bar and slips side to side
so her jumpingstick legs can tap the pedals. Her hands reach
out to hold the handlebars. Her grandmother, babushka round
and heavy as stone, stands behind a picket fence watching the
child reining the bike.

This little girl high and consummate on her high horse bike,
she has come out to play. She sidles up beside me and we pedal
together splashing through the mud.

"Hel—lo." She breathes it out. She speaks halting, exact Russian English. It is a gift she knows she must not squander.

She is small and beautiful gliding on the bar gliding her bike
beside me. She has the breeze lifting her eyelashes and a yellow
ribbon feathering back through her braid.

"Hello."

She laughs completely. She has been huffing up and down
glancing over impatiently for an answer. All her life she has
been a little girl on her high horse bike.

"Hello!" She trills it. It is only a word to her in a strange
language and it makes her laugh. She is unafraid. She
knows nothing of any other moment. Mortality cannot touch
her.

"*Kuda ty yedish?*" I say. Where are you going?

I think she might want to talk but she doesn't. She is riding.
She is riding with me and that is more than we could have ever
imagined.

We ride together. She is above the mud and I am with her so
I am too.

Then we are already to the edge of the village, still in sight of
her grandmother. The babushka has waddled through the gate
and stands in her rubber boots with her man hands on her cow
hips. She shouts.

The little girl turns her face to me. Her braid is snapping and
the ribbon is streaming and her toes are barely touching the
pedals.

The babushka shouts again.

I do not understand. I look back. The babushka is standing
in the mud beside her blue picket fence. She looks like a bear.
She has her arm out straight pointing past us and past the
cabins.

The little girl stops pedaling and lets her legs swing out. She throws her head back. She coasts, arcing away slowly as if she were a kite. She smiles to me over her shoulder and I hear the babushka.

"*BALOTA.*"

2

I GOT my first bike when I was five. It was red and I had it for one summer. Then it was stolen in the fall lying in flying yellow leaves in the front yard.

I had been invalided by a stranger. To me it was as if I were suddenly just like old Mr. Schicksal. He was shot in the back. "One fine Russian boy with a mother," he said. He spoke with a heavy accent and wanted to hold my hand when I got too close. He lived with his faraway eyes crumpled in a stickwood wheelchair holding him and his medals very still in his backyard with his rosebushes growing tall as trees.

My parents didn't have money for another bicycle. I had to wait six years. Until I had a paper route and had strode the journey in the dark before school for five months and could split the cost with my Dad.

For six years I was condemned and I knew it. But the summer I was five, I was set free.

It wasn't my birthday and it wasn't Christmas. It had rained in the night and I was jumping on the sidewalk splashing ants. I didn't see my Dad come around behind me. I was up in the air quick, his hand over my eyes and that smell he dabbed me with before Sunday school smothering me and his scratchy chin against my ear kissing the side of my head.

"Mark David I have a surprise." My Mom was beaming and

15

my Dad never called me Mark David unless I was in trouble so I was confused. I can't remember where Steve and Pam were. Maybe they were playing inside.

"Close your eyes." My Mom was young then and so beautiful but I didn't know it until I was looking at snapshots of me and her when I was fifteen and high on hormones. My Dad was in graduate school in mathematics. He spanked and hugged passionately and wore thickframed glasses that I didn't know were so goofy until I found them in a shoebox and wore them to a party.

I closed my eyes. I wanted to look but I knew I couldn't because those were the rules. My eyes were straining through my eyelids. Then I felt one of his immense hands on my shoulder and something cold press against my wrist. I grabbed it and shouted and my eyes sprang open involuntarily.

I stood there turning pink and gasping and throttling the handlebar grips with red-and-white plastic tassels, but I didn't understand. I didn't know what it was, really. It was elegant and perfect as a colt but I thought it was a toy because it was shiny red with reflectors and grooved tires and a flat white seat. I had seen other kids on bikes but they were other kids older and speaking another language and mean.

"Get on." I climbed up onto the seat. My Mom was watching. My Dad put my soaky shoes on the rubber pedals.

"You have to hold on now. And balance." His hands enveloped mine on the handlebars.

Then I was moving through the grass. Racing fast with the black tires turning dizzily and Dad pushing holding on to the seat. We rushed by Mom and her warm dress and she was waving. We rushed and rushed and then I was leaning sideways falling and Dad was running beside me shouting "balancebalance" and he was leaning over me and I could smell him and he was trying to pull me back up and laughing and shouting "balanceMarkbalance!" but I couldn't help it and I couldn't laugh because I was scared and the wheels slid out and I fell so slowly like when you're waiting for dessert and no one else is done eating yet so you have to wait and we tumbled into the deep grass and I felt Dad over me like a dog and we were giggling.

Dad and I, we practiced. Back and forth beneath the cottonwood trees in Wyoming.

"Oh I forgot. It's easier when you pedal," Dad said. He pumped one of my legs up and down so I could get a feel for it. Mom brought out sandwiches and Steve and Pam to watch but they got bored so she took them and the full plates back inside.

"We want to work at this," Dad said, we got damp and sweaty falling into the grass.

"You'll get it," Dad said, and I believed him.

It was dark when we stopped. Dad bounded up the front porch steps through the screen door. Steve and Pam were already put to bed. I'd been waiting fearfully, looking for my Mom to come out into the hot dark and tell my Dad it was past my bedtime but she never did so I was burning with being a grown-up.

"Just see." Dad pulled my Mom outside by her hand. The moonlight was caught up in the giant trees like tinsel.

I clambered on, anxious and resolute and concentrating. I pushed off and began spinning the pedals furiously and somehow jigglejerked across the grass. I think my Mom was surprised because while I was riding she ran out to me but Dad yelled through the dark, "Don't touch him. He can do it!" So she just trotted alongside looking very happy and worried.

The next day I was still nervous but Dad had to study so Mom pushed me around the house. She pushed me through the grass and held me up when I was a little off balance until I remembered Dad shouting and told her I could do it by myself.

I wibblewobbled in the yard for a few weeks never going farther or faster than I could have gone on foot. Eventually I learned how to balance. I learned what that meant inside my body.

Then I learned how to balance without pedaling. That was something, like floating but you didn't need water.

I zoomed around Steve and Pam to make them laugh or cry. I romped over the erupted sidewalk trying for a squirrel or a bird. I charged bulging roots and got caught halfway and fell over and scraped myself and Mom said it served me right if I wasn't going to be careful, but smiled.

Then one day I went beyond our backyard. Beyond all that I knew down the sidewalk past where we would turn to go give old Mr. Schicksal a casserole. I had been planning it in bed or

maybe dreaming it. I knew I wasn't supposed to but I just had
to see. I went fast in a blur, my great little rabbit heart rejoicing
in my throat. I was liquid, hurling my red bike. I didn't know
how I could go so fast. I didn't know how I could go so far so
fast. I saw giant foreign houses and giant foreign fences all so
near I could have touched them. I smelled new things and
heard strange dogs. I saw foreign kids and foreign Moms all up
close as if they could have lived where I lived. I went to the edge
of the earth. To where looking back I could just make out the
trees in our front yard. Then I almost ran into a car. I stomped
backward on the pedals and squealed and skidded.

Panting, scared, I wheeled around and rode back home crazy
with glory and triumph. That is when I understood.

Thenceforth I was free. I rode far up our dark alley, only
turning around at the sound of dogs and teeth and a chain
rattling as if it weren't connected. I searched out mud and flung
myself through it. I went illegally across the street when Mom
was inside sewing. I scratched my shorn head cruising beneath
old Mr. Schicksal's "sanguine Deutschland roses."

I felt sorry for kids who had to ride in their Dad's car and
couldn't squish dog shit and smell it on their wheels. Or feel
speed and howling in their ears. Or hear the tiny sounds the
grass made. Or fall going fast and in midflight do something
right and land surprised and unhurt and a hero. Those kids
they were trapped. They could never go directly to an anthill or
dead squirrel. They were sealed behind glass and metal inside
vinyl air going somewhere else. They were inside and I was
outside so I was lucky. I was emancipated even from myself:
from my little legs and my little mind. Me on my bike, I could
go anywhere. Anywhere I dared go. I careened and dodged
and penetrated. I, alone, flew and for one boundless summer
made my own plan and carried it through.

Then one fall day I leapt off my bike, ran up the porch and
through the screen door. I had a sandwich and a bowl of soup.
Then I ran back outside to explore my earth and immediately
fell back crying in horror and pain as if I'd been shot in the
back.

3

THAT'S HOW a long journey begins. Long before you could know it.

On another fall day decades later, a blue letter landed on my desk. It wasn't addressed to me. The date was smudged and the stamp hanging off. By all rights it should have been redirected or ambushed or just lost like all those messages in all those bobbing bottles that never made it to shore and would have changed your life completely if they had. But this one made it, faithfully riding the current of unknown hands and unseen machines to wash up on a bank of books.

I opened it, read the first line:

SIBERIAN PASSAGE

and slowly sat back in my chair.

Ever since I was ten and started falling headfirst into maps, Siberia had been the biggest hole. I had been stunned by a world map that spread across one full wall of the county library. It was a Mercator projection so Siberia alone, fabled and green and utterly blank, was colossal, appearing to account for half of the earth's land mass. The volume of mystery shuddered my milky boy mind.

When I got older and had scrabbled around the world some,

Siberia became only more enigmatic. I realized the land had been entombed for decades. There'd been the few straitjacket junkets for avaricious businessmen and diplomats in which everyone, including the multitude of dissolute chaperons in dark sunglasses, drowned themselves in Stolichnaya and caviar; and there was the bleak Trans-Siberian Railroad shunting metal boxes across a region five times the size of Europe—but no one had *traveled* in Siberia. To travel you had to go slow. So slow it seemed as if you weren't even moving, as if you were there. So slow the land would put a thumbprint in you whether you wanted it or not. Siberia remained unexplored, the last dark continent.

For three years I had been trying to inveigle anyone in the octopusal Soviet bureaucracy to let me bicycle in Siberia. I'd spoken to boarfaced apparatchiks and sent sycophantic letters and paid for terse telexes and had *nyet nyet nyet!* shoved down my throat. Now, simply lying on my desk, was a press release from one Carl Jones, documentary filmmaker, stating he'd obtained permission to make a film of

> the first attempt to cross the Soviet Union by bicycle, a five-month, 7,500-mile journey from Vladivostok to Leningrad.

I had never heard of Carl Jones. I dialed the number on the letter.

"I'm sure you understand we have many applicants."

I began listing the countries I'd bicycled through and expeditions I'd been on and stories I'd written.

"Why don't you send me a few of those."

I sent a story about bicycling through South Africa, a tale of pedaling in the Eastern Bloc, and a parable about failing on Mount Everest.

A month later Carl called me. He'd just returned from Russia.

"You're on—got a pen—this is the team. Americans—you, a fellow named Tom Freisem from Seattle and a woman I haven't decided on yet. Russians—two brothers from Siberia, Fyodor and Pavel Konyukhov, and two women, Tanya Kirova and Natasha Traviynskay. I'll send you their addresses."

"What about money?" I said. "I found a bicycle manufacturer in Wisconsin. They'll give us the bikes."

"Good. Get enough for the Soviets."

"And tents? Sleeping bags. Panniers."

"Right. Whatever. You won't need a penny in the country. A Soviet film company is sponsoring everything. In fact they're going to pay each of you three rubles a day. They figure that's enough to live on in Siberia."

I could hear him laughing.

"Mark, all you have to do is ride your bicycle a third of the way around the world. Why don't you write Tom."

Tom Freisem wrote me. His script was neatly jostled. He was writing from the bridge of a fishing vessel in the Gulf of Alaska.

"The frames should be steel rather than aluminum so we can arc weld them in the field if necessary . . . must rig them with drop handlebars to foil the head winds . . . thin tires and strong rims are essential . . . as for drive trains, mud will definitely . . ." The letter went on for four pages.

We met only once, at seven in the morning in a roadside restaurant. It was raining and we were both hungover. We shook hands and ordered eggs and orange juice. Neither of us could eat the eggs. I got down the toast and Tom had more coffee and after a while our brains, like flooded engines, started choking and coughing and coming back to life.

"Have a look at a map yet?" Tom said.

"Yup."

"Big." He put a fork in his cup and began stirring.

"The biggest."

"Eight time zones. Twice the distance from New York to L.A."

"Did you notice the part above Manchuria?"

Tom grinned. "Lucky aren't we!" His eyes looked like little blue moons. *That's* why it's never been done."

Tom didn't look like a cyclist. He had the physique of a high school basketball player—elbowy, thin neck, flat shoulders, curly blond head. I knew everything was going to be fine.

Good travelers don't look like marines. That's just the myth. You meet some guy who has walked across deserts sailed unnamed seas survived harrowing untold hardships, and you expect him to be taut as a wire and taciturn with weathered wise blue eyes . . . and the guy has a paunch and perfectly normal eyes and loves to laugh and talk and drink and you couldn't pick him out of a crowd of derrick hands because the sinew is all inside.

Tom was a Yankee. After getting a degree in German he left New England to visit a friend in Seattle, and stayed. He got a job in a bookstore. He quit to work in a Greek restaurant where he met a fish broker, a man who bought and sold fish at sea. Tom asked him for a job. The man said no.

Then one day the man called. "You wanna job yer ass's gotta be up in Shelikhov Strait in twenty-four hours."

Tom had never been to sea. Shelikhov Strait is the rough black water between Kodiak Island and the Aleutian Peninsula. That first stint was ninety-two days straight on a Korean fishing vessel directing the loading and unloading of thousands of tons and millions of dollars of pollock.

Later he worked on Polish ships. He learned Polish. He learned how to sleep when the ship was jouncing like a cork. He learned how to forget about any freedom beyond a floating metal tub. He learned how to stay awake on his feet at the bridge for thirty-six hours with his bony throat at the radio directing cranes and men with snow falling and everyone scared and the ocean kicking the ships like they were plastic toys.

"So how'd you end up on this thing?"

"I bicycled across the U.S."

"Where to where?"

"Seattle to Boston. Rode right into Massachusetts Bay, stood there in the water, and thought, What next?"

"When was this?"

"Summer 1981."

I smiled.

"What?"

"I rode across the U.S. that summer."

"Where'd you wind up?"

"Massachusetts Bay."

Tom gave me a crinkly, happy look as if he'd expected this.

Then we talked about equipment. In one hour, scribbling on our napkins, we determined what a team of seven would need to bicycle across Russia. Duct tape to baling wire to spare ball bearings.

"You know Africa's been crossed," Tom said as he got up.

"I know."

"And South America and China and Europe. India. Australia."

I nodded.

"This is the last great ride."

The next time I saw Tom was in Nakhodka, a Siberian port city on the Pacific Ocean.

Nine months later the American woman cyclist Carl had chosen dropped out. Tom was already in Nakhodka with the Konyukhov brothers. It was three days before Carl and I and this woman were to fly to Moscow. Tom had had a hunch this might happen and left a message,

Carl: Anything goes wrong, invite Torie. She's a horse.

Victoria that is, Victoria Scott. Tom had told me about her. She too was a Yankee. Old-Irish-sailed-to-New-England-settled-in-Vermont blue blood. She escaped to the West Coast when she was young, became a vegetarian, got an M.A. in Faulkner. She lived in Seattle. She worked as a masseuse and read rapaciously and believed in peace and socialism. She had her favorite macramé-and-fern breakfast spots, commuted on a bicycle and got groceries on a bicycle and went to foreign movies on a bicycle.

She and Tom were riding partners. They trained together, fast for fifty miles through the rain. Tom said she had legs. And that's how he put it to Carl so Carl would understand. Carl was a filmmaker, he'd never traveled by bicycle. He didn't understand.

Carl called Torie the next morning. With two days notice, Torie quit her job, packed up her life and left her girlfriend to go on a bike ride.

The three of us flew to Moscow on June 10, 1989.

4

THE HOTEL was a mazelike mausoleum one block from Red Square. All the rooms down all the dark corridors were the same: a bad TV, a good bed, a deep tub, and two shoe brushes. On top of the TV was a round, wooden, cold-faced Matrioshka doll. There was no toilet paper and no soap.

"These are luxuries my friend. Toilet paper and soap and sugar and coffee and meat."

It was eleven in the morning. I was sitting with a stranger in the hotel buffet. He said he was a salesman from Irkutsk. He was balding with a blunt chin. He looked like the kind of man who could grow a beard in a morning. He'd invited me to his table for crackers and caviar.

"My God boy, don't eat the hotel food." He didn't say where he learned his English. He didn't have an accent. He squeezed red caviar from a tube.

"It is quite simple. If you are an ordinary Soviet citizen, such as myself," he smiled, his whiskers like tiny shards of blue metal, "that is, not a member of the Communist party, that is one with, shall I say, inadequate friends and relatives, you need a coupon to purchase such items, officially, of course. Unofficially, you need only something the store manager needs. Or, wants."

"Like what?"

He had his head back. He had a thick neck. He was staring at the ceiling. "Needs and wants. Wants and needs. It can be easy to get them confused, can it not."

I didn't answer.

"Oh, for instance, condoms." He lowered his head and popped a thick, caviar-loaded cracker into his mouth. He chewed loudly. He watched me watch him, stood up, went over to the buffet and brought back two water glasses. He took a bottle of vodka out of his briefcase and filled both glasses to the brim. He squirted little caviar castles onto two more crackers, handed me one, and made a toast.

"To your education."

We ate and drank. We talked. When I got up to go, misstepping, he grinned. "Perhaps you may try your floor lady. But remember my friend, money means nothing here. Money is not power. Giving money does not mean you will get what you want. *My* country is not so simple."

The floor lady was a terminally sleepy woman who sat at a desk all day and all night. All hotels in all communist countries have floor ladies. They guard keys to the rooms on their floors like dogs. They might be friendly like friendly dogs and they might be mean like dogs you want to shoot. My floor lady was friendly. I gave her an American T-shirt and she found soap and toilet paper and forced me to let her press my pants.

The three of us spent four days in Moscow waiting for a flight to Vladivostok. During the day I investigated the city by bike. At night I got to know Torie.

"Faulkner?"

It was late. We were in my room sitting on the bed. We were sharing beers I got on the black market. Torie was staring at me. Her face was small and diamond-shaped. She had short blond hair cut in a pageboy. She had one eyelid that grew tired before the other. Her eyes were little-girl-never-missing-a-thing green eyes.

She nodded gravely. "All the sound and the fury."

We'd long since covered the usuals, art and Marx and sex. The windows were clotted with rain. Lightning periodically spilled purple across the room. It was muggy.

"Actually, lately I have been reading travel writing. Good travel writing is quite rare you know." Her back was against the wall. She'd slipped her shoes off to curl her legs underneath her.

"Don't read it much," I said.

"You should."

"Why?"

"For the journey."

"I'm on a journey."

She smirked. She was disappointed in me, again. "Listen Marco, the best travel writing, the literature of travel, is capable of transporting you better than if you were to go there yourself."

"I don't want it to be better than if I go myself."

"You're a prick."

I shrugged.

"You know. When I first met you I thought you were going to be some kind of cowboy asshole."

"I thought we'd been getting along pretty well."

"We have. And you are." She smiled. She had a horse-teeth smile.

We were down to our last two bottles of beer. I was drunk.

"But . . . fiction is still better. It's truer." She was staring at me again.

"No such thing."

"What?"

I took a drink.

"No such thing as fiction?"

"Yup."

Torie laughed nervously. She looked at me carefully. "And nonfiction?"

"Nope."

Her eyes were soft and confused.

"Torie?" My voice was gravelly. "Have you ever been to a communist country before?"

"No."

Three hours later we met in the hallway. I'd suggested we take a morning walk about Moscow. Our internal clocks were flipflopped so I knew she wouldn't be sleeping.

The floor lady was fast asleep, her gray hair tumbled over her face and her cheek wrinkled on the desk. We slipped into the elevator and sank down to the lobby. The doorman, dusty, smoking steadily and sleeping, heard us coming and raised one misshapen eyelid. Ashes were spilled down his suit coat. He didn't open the door.

Outside it was murky. The pavement was puddled with large dark stains. They looked like moles. The cement buildings were shrouded. We walked down a narrow street, then hooked right going north along the Moscow River.

Across the coagulated water we could see old tenements with enormous placards, prototypical proletariat placards: red androgynous worker eternally hammeringweldingscything. The old tenements leaned against perfectly cloned new tenements leaning against a factory with broken windows leaning against a bombed-out church. City sweet-and-sour, wet cement and smog and smoke from factories humming and crashing through the night, poured into our mouths. It was only a short walk but Torie's eyes had grown.

"God!" she whispered.

"Communism different in Seattle?"

"Go to hell."

"Why did you come here Torie?"

We kept walking.

"Mark, I'd have to go back to my first bike."

I nodded.

We were strolling through the largest city in Europe on an early warm summer morning and no one was alive. No joggers no dog walkers no cat watchers with noses pressed lightly against the window. There were no messy markets with mustached ladies singing and stacking fish. No canopied carts with outrageous slogans. No cupboardlike stalls beside the river waiting for their odd little owners to appear with a cup of coffee and a murder mystery and the inability to sell anything at all. No graffiti no garish advertising no garbage. No neon light no made-up girls bound home for a day of night. No bagladies.

"I feel like I'm underwater," Torie said. "As if . . ."

As if we'd been pushed out of a plane over an unknown ocean and fallen through a foreign sky and hit the surface softly and sunk down and down and down. Under here everything was distorted from the immense weight of water. You could feel it against your chest. Things were dark and in slow motion. They could roll upside down, or lean preternaturally, or float forever.

We turned up through Red Square. It was vacant. The Kremlin was dark and misty with ridiculously high walls, hiding inside what I suppose all medieval castles have to hide in the twentieth century. There was a great red flag with His face—sharp goatee, bald head, leering eyes—draped over one wall.

St. Basil's Cathedral was opposite the Kremlin. When a lady appeared at the church gate, we paid and went in.

At once I felt as if somehow, through a tunnel or secret door, we had actually passed into the Kremlin. The church was a castle. A maze. Narrow brickthick passages linking one dank chamber to the next, like something thought up by an evil Escher. All the chambers were small and round with a distant vaulted ceiling. On the ceilings were flying devils or saints, all with strange, contorted bodies. The chambers were so dark and indistinguishable, it was easy to get disoriented. Torie managed to spin through the cathedral twice before I found her.

"This is a church?" She had her back against a wall and her hands pressed against the stones. She was staring upward.

"How could people ever gather and sing, or pray?" Her voice did not echo or rise. This scared her.

"Mark, this is a church with no sanctuary."

5

CARL HAD ASKED us to come to his room that evening. When I arrived his door was open and he was shouting into the phone.

"They're not here yet?" Torie walked in with her hips thrust forward, feet turned in, hands in her hip pockets. She dropped into a chair beside the bed.

Carl was cursing. He slammed down the phone and turned to Torie. They started talking about food. It was one of their pet conversations.

"I can't believe what they eat!" said Torie.

"It is revolting isn't it," said Carl. Torie and Carl were devout vegetarians. In three days they had refused to eat many things.

Our first evening in Moscow we'd been invited to the home of a composer. He was a friend of Carl's, a big single man with a picture of Duke Ellington above his piano. He'd spent the day preparing the meal. When he carried out the main course—cabbage stuffed with meat—he was red and humble and sweating with pride. Torie and Carl refused the dish. They filled up on the hors d'oeuvres and then each had two helpings of ice cream.

"I've been one for eleven years," Torie was saying. Carl said he was just starting. The conversation went on. I said nothing. I was thinking about what the man in the buffet had said.

"Mark?" Carl looked at me. "What do you say?"

"Omnivore," I said.

Then there was a knock at the door. Carl sprang from his chair.

"Come in, come in." He swept his arm toward Torie and me and we popped to our feet.

"Let me introduce Natasha Traviynskay."

I stepped forward, spoke my name and stuck out my hand. Natasha shook it hard, once, and let go. Torie had her arms in a rectangle across her chest. She waved hello with her fingers.

Natasha did not smile. She stood with her back straight. She wore a blue polyester dress. Her hair was blond and short, sticking out every which way like the hair on a little girl's doll. Her lips were unpainted and pooched as if she were mad. She was very pretty.

Only after Carl motioned her to the bed did she move. She walked stiffly. She had a hard body. It occurred to me that Natasha Traviynskay looked the way I imagined the stereotypical female Soviet athlete would look, like a male. Not the face, she had a beautiful childlike face, but the muscled, robot body.

On the plane Carl had told me he'd found Natasha via a TV campaign in Moscow. He and his Soviet partners ran a commercial urging women to apply for a "historic adventure." Carl had interviewed dozens of women. He said he was looking for "someone who looks good on film."

"She doesn't speak English," Carl said.

I caught Natasha's eyes when he said this. She understood.

Torie fished phrases from a pocket dictionary and I intentionally mangled the words hoping to get Natasha to smile, but she didn't. When the questions came out decipherable, she answered, in Russian. How old are you? Twenty-three. What is your occupation? Swim coach. Where do you live? Moscow. When we asked something she didn't want to answer, she sat stone-still looking at each of us, one at a time, moving her eyes not her head.

Just as the silence was becoming painful, as if on cue, another knock.

"Come in," Carl said.

A woman slipped into the room. She hurried to the bed, sat down beside Natasha and apologized.

"Sorry for late." She bowed her head. "I just finish architecture exam." Her hair was the color of sand, jagged and professionally coiffed. She wore pink eye shadow.

"Tanya Kirova," Carl said, inexplicably pleased with himself.

Tanya Kirova had voluptuous legs. She crossed them while everyone watched. She wore designer jeans with zippers at the ankles and sat sideways with her rear up a little. She was buxom. She looked furtively around the room. She had one braceleted hand in her lap and the other hidden inside a bucketlike leather purse she'd set on the bed beside her. Her fingernails were long and pink. She'd had a manicure.

Natasha didn't look at Tanya. They had never met. Sitting side by side on the bed, it was obvious they hated each other instantly.

Tanya was fidgeting. She still had her hand inside the purse. "It's OK," Carl said.

Tanya blinked at us coyly. Her hair was in her eyes. The hand inside the purse jerked. She broke into an uneasy smile, wet her lips and lifted a large black rat from the purse.

The animal squirmed in her pink fingernails and Tanya giggled. She set the rat down on the bed.

"This is Felix," she squealed.

For a moment the rat lay immobile on its stomach. It was long and narrow and neckless, tiny black claws, pointed head, bulbous eyes and puffy black balls below a scaly tail.

Tanya was looking at us then looking at her rat then looking back at us when the animal suddenly raced over her legs, up across her chest and stopped on her shoulder. It rose on its hind legs for a moment, then scampered along her collarbone and dropped into the neck of her blouse.

Tanya giggled again. She had sharp teeth with spaces in between. Carl grinned. Torie pretended to laugh. Natasha's face remained blank, her eyes searching the wallpaper above our heads.

The rat poked around inside Tanya's blouse. You could see a dark mound rise between her breasts and then disappear. Tanya would twist and dip her shoulders as if she were being tickled. She seemed absorbed, entertained.

Carl had also spoken about Tanya on our flight. He said he'd picked her because she was "quite different. Unusual, know what I mean. She'll make a good character. Got a hell of a bod too," he'd motioned lewdly with his hands. "I don't give her a month. A month at most. But that'll be some good dirt for the film."

The rat was still inside Tanya's blouse.

"Felix is my pet," she said. She explained that many of her friends had rats for pets. "Moscow is a good place for rats."

She untucked her blouse and let the rat crawl out onto her knee. She stroked its back while it sniffed the hotel air.

No one had spoken. Natasha was still scrutinizing the wallpaper.

"I am sorry," Tanya said. "He does not eat very much. He will eat anything."

Torie and I didn't understand.

"I take him with us, yes?"

I quickly looked at Carl. He was amused. "Of course you can!"

Torie concurred. I kept shut. I was thinking *Jezzus Christ*. Natasha's face was calm. Her eyes blank.

Suddenly the rat spun backward, scuttled up onto Tanya's breasts, clung there looking right and left, then leapt heavily into Natasha's lap.

Natasha caught her breath. The rat looked up at her with tremorous black eyes. Natasha looked down with her neck rigid.

"He does not bite," Tanya said.

Natasha slowly moved her hand over the top of the rat and touched it with her fingertips.

"He is a smart rat," Tanya said.

Body squatting, eyes fixed like dark seeds, claws gripping the folds in her skirt, Felix the rat pissed in Natasha's lap. He made a warm dark stain. Then he scampered over the bed and back up onto Tanya's shoulder.

6

IN THE MORNING the five of us flew to Vladivostok. We were met
at the airport by a group of men in dark suits. Carl did not
know them but they said they were part of the film crew. We
were immediately bused up the coast to Nakhodka. We were
told our journey would begin there.

"Why?" I asked one of our chaperons. He was young with
active eyes and didn't belong in a suit.

"This is an irrelevant question."

I didn't say anything.

"You are an American. You are going to ask me 'Why is this
an irrelevant question?' and I am going to tell you this too is an
irrelevant question."

When we arrived in Nakhodka, Carl disappeared with the
dark suits in search of his real camera crew. The rest of us went
to dinner in the hotel dining room.

It was a formal dining room. The drapes looked like taffy.
We were given large menus. We perused the entrées then tried
to order. The waitress grimaced as if someone had pinched her
calves. Tanya spoke with her, then turned to us.

"It is what I thought, they make only one thing here. The
menu is just for to look at. You see in our country . . ."

The clap of the dining-room doors interrupted her. In came

Tom striding across the wood floor. Behind him were two men.

"Damn, they let you in did they." He slapped me on the shoulder. "You look better than the last time I saw you." He stepped over and hugged Torie.

"Well now, I just figured it'd work out."

"Tanya Kirova, Natasha Traviynskay—Tom Freisem," I said.

Tom wiped the bicycle oil onto his pants and gave each of the women a warm handshake.

"Team bike mechanic," he said laughing. "Now, allow me to introduce Fyodor and Pavel Konyukhov."

The two brothers stepped forward. They were smallish, skittish, hairy men. They were solemn. They shook hands hard as if it were a contest. Neither said a thing. Tom made further introductions in Russian, then we all sat down.

The brothers Konyukhov did and did not resemble each other. They both had dense beards and long, straggling, headbanded hair. Both were short and lean and clad uncomfortably in polyester shirts and pants. Each wore a dirty string around his neck. On the string was an animal tooth.

When the soup came they set right to it, slurping vigorously, their hair almost in their bowls. At one point, Fyodor looked up at me, pulled a business card from his pocket, and handed it across the table. One side was in Russian, the other in English.

KONYUKHOV
FYODOR FILIPPOVICH

The USSR Artists' Union Member
Wearer of the Peoples Friendship Order,
Honoured Master of Sports of the USSR
Traveller, Participant of Ski Expeditions to the
Pole of Inaccessibility of 1986, USSR—North Pole
Canada of 1988, Autonomous crossing to the North Pole
of 1989, Cycle—Race Vladivostok—Leningrad of 1989

The last item I found curious. Our bike ride, which was not to my knowledge a race, which hadn't even begun, was already on the card. I looked at Tom.

"Fyodor is thirty-seven," he said. "He's been doing expeditions for twenty years."

I nodded. "I see he likes the North Pole."

"Pavel is thirty-two. He's a gym teacher. They're both from this part of Siberia. They don't speak a word of English."

I looked at Pavel to see if he had a business card, but he didn't. He wouldn't look back at me. Instead, when he'd finished his soup, he spoke to Tanya.

"He says he has already bicycled across Russia. On a one-speed–type bicycle and carrying a rucksack," said Tanya.

This shocked me. But, before I could start asking questions, the main course came. It was a gravy-and-meat dish with cucumber salad. Torie cringed. I gave her my salad.

We ate quietly while twilight coated the room. The lights were not turned on. The pillars between the windows cast heavy shadows across the table. I stared at the Konyukhov brothers.

There was something strange. It wasn't their matted hair or their gnarled beards or their peculiar, cautious behavior. I couldn't put my finger on it but I could feel it. Even with my eyes closed I could feel it.

I knew Fyodor felt my gaze, but he kept eating. Only when he had finished the gristle on the bones did he raise his head and look at me. His face was severed in half by a shadow. It was as if there were two completely different sides to him, one inscrutably dark, the other light. His eyes settled on me. They were pale blue, ice-blue eyes. He made no attempt to avert his look.

I glanced at Pavel. He was completely in shadow. He peered up at his big brother, twisting his head and coughing, then slowly lowered his eyes on me. He had impenetrable black blank eyes sunk inside dark rings. His hair reached into his beard.

For a few moments it was as if there were no one else in the room. Just the two Siberians, and me.

My head jerked back to Fyodor. His expression had not changed. His face was still cut in half. Slowly I realized he was looking at me the way a predator looks at its prey. With indefinable, impersonal, mesmerizing contempt. His eyes, light and cool and white blue, were the eyes of an animal. The eyes of a wolf. I had seen it only a few times before, on other expeditions, in men who had been born in the wrong century, men who could live only outdoors, as if civilization itself were a form of unbearable captivity.

Suddenly I knew what I was feeling. The brothers were only briefly caged in their clothes. The ridiculous shoes and synthetic pants were a costume. They were playing the game, humoring everyone by sitting quiet as animals in a zoo. Fyodor and Pavel Konyukhov were wild.

7

We SPENT the next week in the basement of a Nakhodka high school, preparing. We seldom saw Carl.

It was jubilant halcyon business. Gunky monkey serious business. All day bent over your machine tweaking and tightening and testing with *it's gonna happen gonna happen gonna happen* lilting around in your head until you'd catch yourself singing it out loud.

Such is preparing for a journey. That cathartic opportunity to cleave away the mindless weight of possessions, and travel light. The wild chance to reclaim the life of seminal man: man the nomad. Expurgated man. Man for whom aesthetics and ascetics were one.

As the Bedouin with their camels, or the Sioux with their horses, our first concern was our bicycles. Tom and I did much of the work.

Traveling east to west, we would be riding against prevailing winds; hence we replaced the upright handlebars with curved drop bars enabling us to curl over and reduce wind resistance. We relocated the gear shifters from the handlebars down to the down tube to simplify shifting. We exchanged the knobby tires for slicks to gain speed. We mounted fenders for the mud and bolted on racks for our panniers. We oiled every moving ap-

39

pendage, adjusted front and rear derailleurs and attached
watch-size, waterproof, computerized odometers.

One afternoon we split up the group gear. We had two-man
tents. Tom and Torie would bunk together, Fyodor and Pavel,
Natasha and Tanya. I drew a yurt to myself. The few other
group items were also divvied up. Tom and I would each carry
a repair/tool kit. Torie would carry the medical kit, Fyodor the
ax and one cooking pot, Pavel another pot, Tanya the ladle.
Natasha refused to carry anything more than her own gear.

Late in the week I handed out rain jackets, shorts, shirts,
sleeping bags and foam pads. Pavel immediately returned the
sleeping pad.

"*Nyet*," he said.

"*Pachimu?*" I said. Why?

He pulled me over to his corner of the basement and unfastened the string around a tightly bound hide. He spread the
hide on the cement floor and proudly lay down on the dark fur.
I stuck my thumb up and he grinned. Both Tanya and Fyodor
were standing nearby.

"Tanya," I said, "could you ask Pavel for me what it was like
bicycling across Siberia."

She spoke to him.

"He says 'bugs and mud.' "

"Anything else?"

"*Eta fsyo?*"

Pavel spoke quietly.

"He says 'bugs and mud, and then snow.' "

"That's it?"

"*Shto yisho?*"

"*Ah Sibirski tiger.*"

" 'And the Siberian tiger.' " Tanya's voice was a whisper.

I made a face.

Fyodor and Pavel stared at me, their eyes flat.

"Sibirski tiger?" I said.

Their expressions did not change. Pavel spoke and Tanya
translated.

"He says, 'He is out there.' "

Pavel's voice was thin and scratchy. He stood with his hands
down at his sides. He said one morning they had found deep

paw prints in the snow. He said a Siberian tiger could smell a human from three miles away.

"I thought the Siberian tiger was a myth."

Tanya translated this. Fyodor's eyes flared. Pavel spoke but Tanya hesitated.

"Tanya, what did he say?"

"He says: 'You will never see him, but he is there.' He says: 'You will feel him, as though he were inside your skin.'"

The next day Pavel handed me a group of black-and-white photographs. They were from his ride across the Soviet Union. It was winter in the pictures. There were two unidentifiable men inside fur parkas, fur boots and fur mittens, wearing backpacks and pushing bicycles through the snow. The wheels of their bicycles cut grooves in the drifts. They were carrying rifles. Pavel explained how they shot snowshoe rabbits for food. The wind howled. They were in blizzards. One picture showed a bursting purple toe. The more I gawked the more Pavel smiled.

"Thomas, why is he showing *me* all this?" Tom was checking the brakes on his bike by careening back and forth in the basement.

"Forgot to tell you. Last night I told them you were on Everest."

"Jesus."

That afternoon Fyodor brought in his photos. They were from one of his North Pole expeditions. Again all the men were dressed in heavy furs and standing penguinlike in appalling weather. Shunning the use of dogs they had man-hauled six-hundred-pound sleds to the "Pole of Inaccessibility." One man had died, one had broken his back, one had gone mad. Every one of them got frostbite. This was all in the photos. Only a third of them made it to the Pole, Fyodor was one. There was a picture of him there. His wild blue wolf eyes and his black-scabbed nose and his frozen beard.

The night before we left, Pavel introduced me to the man with whom he'd bicycled across Russia. I'd seen this man before. Already there were always unexplained people around us, watching us. We'd gotten used to ignoring them.

Two days earlier, when we were feverishly reaching a point when all the bikes were ridable, this man had brought a home-made lunch down into the basement. In the commotion, his offering had gone largely unnoticed. I had been sweaty and fluish. I'd slept through the hotel breakfast. I ate it.

"Sergei Ravlovich, Mawrk Shinkons," said Pavel.

"Sergei," the man said for himself. His voice was soft. He used only his first name as if somehow we were already friends.

"Mark," I said.

"*My rahn'sha paznakomilis.*" We have met before.

I shook my head. "I don't think so."

"*My apyat' poznakomimsya.*" And we will meet again.

He said this almost sorrowfully. I was perplexed.

He was a short man, a rock. His handshake hurt. He wore starched camouflage fatigues and hard-shined black service boots. His head was triangular and his hair short as mine. His neck was the limb of a tree. He had a red complexion and a strange smile. The kind of enigmatic smile that men who've seen very different things sometimes have. It is warm and sincere and you know you are lucky to get it, but it looks as if it hurts them.

Pavel had his photos nearby. He picked up the pile and shuffled through them. He found the one of the bursting purple toe and pointed to Sergei. I nodded. I wondered if it had been amputated.

"*Sergei parashyutist. Ochin' kharoshi chilavyek.*" Sergei is a paratrooper. He is a good man.

Sergei had not moved. He was standing directly in front of me, staring at me. Pavel went on but Sergei didn't seem to be listening.

Then Pavel stopped. Sergei was slowly undoing the top button of his shirt. I could see the skin of his chest stretched tight. He bowed slightly and pulled a string over his head. I attempted to step back but his face, smiling or frowning, I couldn't tell, stopped me. He placed the string over my head.

I looked down. On the string was a large, yellowed claw. It was hooked and had a glass-sharp point. Bits of gnarled skin and tawny hair clung to the bone.

"*Sibirski tiger,*" he said.

8

W E BACKED our bicycles down the beach until the rear wheels slid into the Sea of Japan. The surf crashed into our legs and washed through the spokes and we whooped because it was icy. Then we mounted and set off across the largest continent on earth.

I was soaring. I had this uncontrollable grandness in me. I could feel the edge of the continent right up through my wheels. I could feel the vast unknownness and the beckoning and the dread because it was the blurry hurry very first fine day of the journey and on the first day of a journey you feel every-thing that might happen to you. You feel it as if it had already happened to you. The sky was runny and the ocean inky and I could smell the highway and hear the forest as if I were only riding my little blue bike but I wasn't, I was gone

gone clear back back up into the plane high up above the planet peering down at the whole inconquerable sea to shining sea watching green going on and on to the fucking ends of the earth euphoria surging in me like lava for the sheer whack thwack boy adventure of it all and at that instant dread fathomless stillborn dread like a sliver of glass you can't see but feel and can't find to pull out because you already know it must work its ownself out the way the journey will because it's always the journey the grand fucking grand thing you planned and dreamed and scammed and schemed with a little faith and a little luck because they're

43

*the same anyway when one day you wake up and shit shit it's the day and
it's inescapable and you have immeasurable kicking joy inside you like
a baby because you are starting something called a journey you have no
idea whether you can even finish or live through and shout at yourself
inside yourself for your hubris and doubt your faith and that is everything just the getting to and beginning the beginning of something
grand and that is the meaning of grandness itself and that is what
humans are meant for, and that is dread.*

We rode through Nakhodka surrounded by a prickly welter
of press cars. Carl's film crew dashed about in a military jeep
shoving the camera and microphone in our faces. We had a
police escort, one cop car in front and one in back. I immediately caught the lead patrol car and tailed it twenty miles to the
top of the first pass. At the summit I tried to plunge myself
down the other side but the police screamed through their
windshield then screeched out in front almost knocking me off
my bike. I rolled up into the pine trees, took a seat, and leered
down at them like a gargoyle.

Tom came up next, followed by Natasha and Torie, then the
brothers, then Tanya (with Felix in her handlebar bag). Behind
Tanya was our entourage: Carl's film jeep, another cop car
howling like a hit dog, a black sharksilent automobile with tinted
windows, and a half-ton supply truck.

Watching our parade from above, I felt sick. This wasn't
a bike ride, this was a circus. One of those old grimy suspect half-burlesque-half-freak-show-here-in-tents-gone-in-the-
morning mysterious gypsy operations. Bizarre acts and tattooed
people and wild animals. Supposedly, we would all be camping
together for months.

When everyone had assembled on the summit, we were carefully lined up with our bicycles and asked to smile big, *"bal'shoy
bal'shoy,"* and wave and wave again. The press snapped and the
TV crew filmed. We were given little red pins and little red flags
and asked to do it all again. We were asked rhetorical questions
and asked to respond properly. You are very fortunate to be
bicycling across Siberia yes we are very fortunate to be bicycling
across Siberia you will see what no one has seen yes we will see
what no one has seen.

Then a fat man in a rumpled suit stepped out of the dark

sharkmobile. He wore dark sunglasses. He walked over to Fyodor and spoke to him in private. Then he made a speech. Everyone was quiet. It was a turgid prolix speech about peace and friendship and workers uniting and He was invoked and hope and goodwill and hands over the sea. Our inordinate bravery was mentioned several times.

We had heard this speech when we arrived in Moscow and when we left Moscow and when we arrived in Vladivostok and at no less than three banquets in Nakhodka.

Tom winked at me. I had made a snide remark under my breath. He wanted me to quit being a horse's ass.

"All gonna pass," he whispered.

"This is way Soviets do things," Tanya said. She was looking straight ahead, her face held in such a way that anyone would have believed she was actually listening to the speech.

The voice of the rumplesuit was so close to a voice from my childhood, the deathdull deliverance of Reverend Pete Lange-weile, minister to the high plains of Wyoming, my mind already had a well-traveled escape path. I fled

to the county library drop my bike kick the snow off my boots bang through the tall doors get a low look get quiet as a book take a huge seat at the oak round table split open The Times Atlas of the World *and pull the heavy pages back one by one to plate 38 and*

relax. Our route. Plain as a string laid across the country. I review the topography, my eyes moving inch by inch east to west. The journey is to be a geographic triptych: the Pacific Ocean to Lake Baikal, Lake Baikal to the Ural Mountains, the Urals to the Baltic Sea.

In the first third we will parallel the northern border of China and then Mongolia. North along the Ussuri River to the city of Khabarovsk; west beside the Amur River through Blagoveshchensk and onward until the road disappears above Manchuria; through whatever there is in that hole in the map until a road reappears; westward still through Chita and Ulan-Ude to Irkutsk on Lake Baikal. I use my hand as a compass swinging thumb-finger-thumb across the region—two thousand miles or more, depending on the roadless region.

In the second third we traverse the West Siberian Plain. From Irkutsk northeast to Krasnoyarsk then due west to Novosibirsk;

westward to Omsk, and across the Irtysh River; steady on to Chelyabinsk at the base of the Ural Mountains. Maybe three thousand miles.

From the top of the Urals we ride down through Kuybyshev to cross the mighty Volga; cruise on to Ryazan; then Moscow, and finally, Leningrad. Another two thousand miles.

"It's too big."

"What?" I blinked. Tom was looking at me out the corner of his eye.

"It's too big. The beginning's only the beginning. When it gets tough, they," Tom nodded toward the crowd, "will be gone."

Then the speech ended and we rolled like seven bright marbles down the backside of the mountain. It was steep through the timber. I was in front flying headlong leaning around curves. I refused to brake. Speed pulled tears from my eyes. On a hairpin turn I cut off the lead cop car.

Two hours later, at lunch, I was cornered by Fyodor and Pavel. We were having a picnic in the woods. I was to be reprimanded. The translator for Carl's film crew, a scruffy little man named Sergei, interpreted.

"You must not do that," said Fyodor. His eyes were burning. He was waving his finger in front of my nose.

"What's that?"

"Ride your bicycle ahead of the police car," said Pavel. He was biting his nails.

"Why not?"

"You must not!" said Fyodor. He flexed his forearms. Natasha came over and stood sullenly beside him.

"You must obey the police," barked Pavel.

"Obey?"

"You must obey the police," Fyodor said.

"What are the police doing with us?"

"They are protecting us."

"I see. From what?"

Fyodor and Pavel and Natasha frowned.

"They will be with us all the way to Leningrad."

"I don't think so," I said.

Sergei did not translate this so Fyodor asked what I said and Sergei told him I said OK. The brothers and Natasha walked away. They had lunch with the rumplesuits in the sharkmobile.

Sergei pulled me to one side. "You do know they *will* be with you the whole way. They have always been with everyone who travels here."

"Sergei, everything is not always the way everything always is."

Sergei lit a cigarette. "You are a very American man. It is going to be hard for you to be in my country."

"Is it hard for you?"

Sergei smiled, and nodded.

Later in the afternoon we rode through forested land that could have been in Canada or Germany except for all the military trucks. At one point the lead patrol car stopped and motioned us off the road. The sharkmobile pulled up beside the police car. The occupants talked to each other through their windows, then the same rumplesuit got out. He stood safe behind his sunglasses and made a short speech.

Tanya paraphrased: "He says, 'Stay in a group no stopping no looking no talking no taking photographs.' "

In two miles we began passing a long brick wall. Behind the wall were pre-Revolution brick buildings with tile roofs. The wall and the buildings were dilapidated. There were wooden sentry boxes along the wall and soldiers with rifles standing inside the boxes. There were soldiers everywhere. The military trucks rumbled up and down the road. The patrol car in front wailed continuously and the trucks pulled off and headtucked people scurried out of our way.

I stared over the wall. So did Tom and Torie. Tanya concentrated on riding which was good because she was a poor cyclist and there were plenty of potholes. Natasha was an excellent cyclist and could have steered herself with her legs alone but her head never turned once. Fyodor and Pavel followed behind me. Whenever I looked over my shoulder they were looking at me.

Past the compound we spread out again. Soon I was happily bicycling by myself. The military leviathans were still cruising back and forth. At the beginning of a long hill one of them passed me, but started belching halfway up. It was a passenger truck with a green canvas top, wheels tall as a man. Inside were soldiers sitting with their rifles between their knees.

I ground hard to catch up. The soldiers started shouting. They started waving me on. The hill steepened. The truck had to drop a gear and so did I. The soldiers were all cheering and I was socking the pedals and gaining and gaining. Finally I pulled up along the outside of the truck and grabbed hold with my left hand.

The driver saw me through his rearview mirror and waved and smiled and slowly pulled the truck into the middle of the road to give me room. The soldiers crowded to the corner of the truck.

"*Dobry dyen'. Nyet.* Good afternoon, sir," said one boy.

They were all boys. Brightfaced boys in heavy wool uniforms cradling their rifles at dangerous angles.

"Good afternoon, gentlemen," I said.

They roared with delight.

"Where are you from, sir?" The boy was speaking for all of them. He was hanging out above my head. He spoke English very clearly with little gaps between each word. He was bespectacled with hair so short I could see where the barber had nicked him.

"America."

The soldiers hallooed.

"Where are you going, sir?"

"Leningrad."

The soldiers hooted. One with a brutish face leaned over his friend and shouted, "*Nivozmozhna!*" That is impossible.

"Why?" I said.

"It is too big to bicycle," said the boy.

"Perhaps."

Another soldier was speaking into his ear.

"Sir, we have seen the police, and the black cars. You are bicycling. Why are they with you?"

I was still hanging on to the side of the truck with one hand. I was being pulled up the hill. My grip was beginning to ache.

"To protect us," I said.

The boy translated this for his friends and they howled and he smiled. His smile was like the smile of a girl. He wasn't more than sixteen.

"That is what they say our job is also, to protect," said the boy, leaning wildly over the tailgate.

"From who?" My hand was now on fire.

The boy translated what he had said, and what I said back, and the soldiers pointed to me and began laughing. They got so happy and riled they tried to pull me up into the truck and almost knocked me off my bike.

"What was that place?" I pointed backward.

"That is where we live, sir."

"They wouldn't let us stop there. I guess they don't want us to see what you have." My thumb had slipped off and I was only hanging on by four fingers.

"Of course," said the boy gaily. His comrades were shouldering around him.

"My friends want me to tell you things."

"What things?" My fingers were loosening.

"We have rats in our rooms. Our rooms do not have heat in winter and we do not have enough blankets. We do not have a hospital. There are some days we have the same soup for every meal."

The soldiers were shouting at the boy.

"My friends, they want me to tell you something. Sir, you will never see our country if you have the police and the black cars with you. No one will talk to you."

My fingers were peeling off and I was beginning to fall and starting to pedal violently and suddenly the boy realized I was slipping away and I saw the loss in his eyes and saw

I was that boy once that kid that young shorthair hardbody precocious as Jesus wanting to talk to anyone and asking questions and questions until they give up throwing their hands in the air saying everything is always the same you'll see and I'm thinking and thinking staying up all night thinking

and the truck drifted slowly forward and the boy stood up and screamed.

"Sir, *SIR!* It is not what we have that they do not want you to see. They do not want you to see what we do not have."

9

Two days later I opened my eyes and it was black and I heard a cuckoo bird calling. Cuckoooo cuckoooo.

I crept out of my sleeping bag and out of my tent and stood naked in the forest. I dressed. I stuffed my bag and dropped the tent and loaded my bike by feel. Then I snuck out of camp. Past the cop cars and the sharkmobile and the sleeping tents.

Up on the road the sky was pink and blue and cold. I pulled on a jacket and pedaled away. I guessed I had two hours before they realized I was gone and the police came after me.

The road tunneled through trees then out across fields of mist. The morning was wet and musky. The road rolled. It had no stripe. There were no cars no signs no fences.

I heard a rabbit shuttling through the brush and caught an owl coasting just above the trees. I saw a big-eared fox, silky and red, standing in the road. I quit pedaling. It tilted its head watching me coming, then leapt off.

A herd of milk cows stopped me. The sun was up now, caught in spiked trees like a bright piece of plastic. The cows were bucking across the road, green shit smacking the pavement, bloated udders swinging. They were bound for an open barn up the hillside.

I rode through the mud up to the barn. It had five stalls. The cows went in one side heavy and uncomfortable and out the other side lighter, frolicking and kicking. Inside each stall, sitting on a three-legged stool, was a spherical woman in a white apron. Each woman wore a white kerchief with a few strands of brown or blond or gray hair falling out but most of it pushed carefully up underneath.

The cows romped in muddy circles nuzzling each other until a stall was empty. Then a woman in a flowing raincoat would charge in with a stick, scatter the beasts, narrow in on one and poke it toward the stall. The animal would lower its head and blast clouds from its nostrils and step up into the stall.

Then the woman on the stool would begin stroking its belly and cooing. The cow would relax. The woman would press her forehead against its large stomach, her woolen legs spread under the white apron and her feet flatfooted on the planks, and gently begin jugging up and down. I could hear the rhythmic plopping.

When the pail was full, and lifted up onto the rail, and the cow shooed forward like a big clumsy little girl, the woman would drop her hands in her lap, turn sideways and watch the dawn.

Another woman, using a yoke with a hook on either end, hoisted the pails off the rail and carried them to a metal tub. She emptied the pails into a sagging sheet spread over the tub. The sheet was held taut by another woman, her round belly pressed up against the rim of the tub.

I zigzagged through the heaving steaming creatures and stopped beside the woman standing at the tub. I put my feet down in the mud and held my bike between my legs and yanked off a waterbottle.

"*Malako mozhit' byt?*" I held my empty waterbottle out to her.

She looked at me and pulled the sheet off the milk. Vapor rose from the tub into her face. She took the bottle, plunged it into the milk up to her elbow, and held it under until the bubbles stopped. Then she pulled it up dripping, wiped it off with her apron, and handed it back to me.

"*Peytye!*" she said. Drink.

The bottle was warm in my hand. The milk tasted thick and rich as blood. I could feel the liquid running hot inside me and smell the sun on the manure and hear the hooves plopping in the mud and the silence of the cuckoo birds and the sirens.

*   *   *

In camp this morning I received a lecture from the rumple-suits about my escape yesterday morning.

"We are here to protect you."

This one had a pocked face. He spoke English. He spoke very politely. He was the one who had looked at the milk woman with his slits for eyes and asked for her address. The woman had stood by her tub of milk with her arms crossed. She had looked right at him, and said nothing.

"We are protecting you."

I looked at his neck and his ears.

"You don't understand our country."

"I know that. That is why I am here."

"You must always stay on the road."

"I would like to see the villages."

"There is nothing in the villages."

"Fuck you."

I snatched my bike back and hurled myself away, quickly catching up with Tanya. She had been riding slow watching the scene over her shoulder.

For a long time we just pedaled side by side. Felix was still riding in her handlebar bag, eating all day, getting fat. We passed Natasha and the brothers, Tom and Torie. When we were out in front, she started talking.

It is difficult to ride beside Tanya and converse because she is a poor cyclist and will look over at you when she is speaking and forget she's on a bicycle. But she is good to talk to, so this morning we were riding together.

Tanya talked about what she always talked about, what every Russian talks about.

"Back then . . ." She was huffing. She was not fit enough to be riding and talking at the same time.

"Back then everyone knew someone who had vanished." She meant back in her father's time. Her father was old, he was a retired physicist. He had married a young strong Jewish woman who was now an old timid Jewish woman.

"It was not unusual," she said, "it was our country." We slowed so she could catch her breath.

"It would happen at night." I suddenly noticed how strong her accent was. I had grown used to it.

"Maybe it would be your father, or your brother. A father or
a brother who spoke his mind. You would plead with him to
forget and be quiet and please just forget and he would speak
his mind anyway.

"And then, always at night in the dark, voices and screaming
and blood and then nothing."

"I can't imagine it," I said.

"But it isn't like that anymore."

"It isn't."

"No . . . But we Russians, we know. We know that history
repeats itself in Russia. It is our heritage." She reached down
and pulled off a waterbottle and almost crashed into me. Her
waterbottle was empty. Tanya regularly forgot to fill her waterbottles in the morning.

"Sorry, mine are empty too," I said.

"You never forget."

"I know."

Tanya looked over at me, then quickly back at the road.

"I will go with you today."

We were riding well ahead of the pack. We could see the lead
patrol car. We slowed down. Fyodor and Pavel and Natasha
passed us, then Torie and Tom. We kept slowing. The distance
between us and the others increased. The tail cop car appeared
behind us. We kept slowing. It didn't know what to do. We kept
slowing, as if we were tired and couldn't keep up. Finally the car
jumped around us and sped ahead.

At the next dirt road, we scanned the highway in both directions, and turned off.

It was a rough road. It went through a coppice and across a
lumpish field before I began to hear a well squeaking and a pig
squealing and sheep baaaaing. Children laughing. Then we
were in a village.

There were little log cabins all around us, each with gingerbread around its windows. The gingerbread was different on
every home—blue or yellow or orange, scrolled or geometrical
with stars and squares or carved into animals.

Shouting kids on big bikes swooped around us swift as pi-
geons. Ragged runnynose children fluttered to catch up. Tanya
asked them where we could get milk. They flung out their
hands in different directions, surprised themselves and started

laughing. Then, bunched close, they began walking us toward a dwarfish cabin.

Enormous tomato plants filled the space between the picket fence and the cabin. The cabin had three crooked windows opening on the mud street, each with a pot of red geraniums. The gingerbread was curious, two birds with their mouths open, facing each other on top of each window.

Tanya knocked on the gate. No one came. The rabble pushed out a tiny boy with torn shorts and oversized suspenders. He looked as if he were about to cry. He stuck his hand up through the slats in the gate, pulled a string and went inside. The kids surrounding us waited silently. They were worried for us.

Then an old woman hobbled out from behind the cabin. She wore a quilted skirt, heavy wool socks and rubber galoshes covered with dung. The little boy was following her.

The woman's arms were round as fence posts. She folded them and leaned over her gate. She had knobby fingers and dirt under her flat fingernails. She wore a yellow scarf tied behind her head.

Tanya asked if we could buy milk from her. The woman looked us up and down as if we were orphans she were about to bathe. I pulled off my sunglasses and tried to pass muster. That made her smile. She bellowed at one of the children behind us because he was touching our bicycles.

"*Malako?*" She said it as if we wanted milk from her own body.

Tanya began to explain but the babushka interrupted.

"I don't believe you." We were strangers in her village and she had never met strangers. No strangers ever came to Siberian villages. It was impossible.

"We are riding our bicycles across Siberia," Tanya said.

"Your bicycles? Like the children? I don't believe you!"

Tanya nodded.

"I have milk," she said, "but it is old milk, this morning's."

Tanya said that would be wonderful. The babushka's face folded up like wrinkles on a dried apple. She became self-conscious and adjusted her scarf. She twirled around, went back behind her cabin, and returned with a jar big as a small watermelon.

We started to pull the waterbottles from our bikes but the

kids wanted to do it. They tussled and shoved and eventually crowded the plastic bottles on top of the gate post. The old woman puffed a gray hair from her face, pulled the top off the jar, and began pouring.

The kids were watching and we were watching and the babushka was pouring steadily and the milk glowed and lit up all the faces. I could see the six singing birds through the milk and the gigantic tomato plants and the red geraniums and the dusty kids giggling and the babushka pretending to be gruff but happy as an old woman gets pouring her milk for another human when a snapping busting popping and a siren shrieking and everyone jumped and a cop car shot up and almost hit one of the children running away screaming.

No one got out of the car. The windows were rolled up. The siren shut off and the light stopped flashing.

Everyone looked back at the babushka. Her face was ashen but she kept pouring. She would not look at us. We had betrayed her. We were strangers and strangers never came to Siberian villages.

The car sat in front of us. The engine roared and scared the children.

Tanya went to the car and knocked on the glass. The engine roared again. Tanya knocked again. The car slipped into gear and rolled backward across the street, crunching on the ruts. Then the engine was cut.

I looked at the babushka in desperation. She looked at me without a look at all. I was a liar.

I walked over to the car with Tanya. She bent into the windshield and asked them to leave. She asked again politely. A window opened a crack.

"We are here for your safety."

"Thank you, but we do not need your protection, please leave."

"You must leave the village."

"Please go away," Tanya said.

"For your safety, you must leave this village."

"Christ, you fucks." I smashed the hood with my fist.

The window rolled up. The engine started. Tanya and I stepped back and the car sprang away shooting mud against our legs.

When we looked back the babushka was gone and her grandson was pale. He was holding our waterbottles. They were full. The other kids were holding our bicycles. They had blank stares and lips too tight for children. We were traitors to them too.

We pedaled back through the mud out of the village and up onto the highway. The cop car flew out from behind a tree and followed us. After an hour of riding, we caught up with Tom.

"Have a good time?"

"Almost."

The three of us rode quietly together with the tail cop car right behind us. We rode very slow for a long time. We let Torie and the Soviets get miles ahead.

"Marco," Tom said finally, "you ready?"

I nodded. "Chase two rabbits you lose 'em both."

"What does that mean?" said Tanya, but Tom was already riding away.

He pedaled hard. Tanya and I pedaled easy. The cop car stayed behind us. When Tom had disappeared, I eased away from Tanya. She understood now.

The cop car remained behind Tanya just long enough. In the next open stretch where it was difficult to hide, where it was improbable to hide, I dropped off the road.

I lie low in the high grass hiding. I have ditched my bicycle in the reeds in the barrow pit. I lie in uncut hay. It pokes my bare legs.

The geography has changed. The forests and hills are gone, replaced by a swamp, a swamp that spreads out flat in every direction, including behind us, as if it had somehow swallowed even our past. There are floating hayfields in the swamp. Yellow patches of land handtrenched and handhayed. I am lying in such a field.

Behind me are two farmers. They stand in a strip they have scythed. It looks like the bare spot on the belly of a dog that has been shaved for an operation. The haymakers wear white veils across their faces and over their heads because of the bugs. They are leaning on their scythes, the blades hook around their boots like scimitars. They are suspicious. They saw a man on a bicycle on the road and kept scything, swinging twisting lopping stepping. When they glanced back he was gone.

I lie in a hole in the high grass sweating and squashing mosquitoes. The sun is boiling the sky. Now and then I lift my head just above the surface of the grass and check the highway. They have passed by. I know they will come back searching.

After a while my mouth gets dry. My waterbottles are on my bike. As I get up, staying low hunching almost crawling, I spot them and drop flat and shimmy backward, grass gouging my elbows and knees. I lie on my stomach and wait, then raise one eye. The car hums past fast. The blue bulb is off. The heads jerk side to side like puppets. They see only the haymakers and haystacks and the field in the swamp.

When they disappear I stand up, slip into the reeds, retrieve a waterbottle and return to my hole in the hay.

The haymakers saw the car go by. Then they saw me rise up from nowhere, vanish in the barrow pit, step back out into the high grass, wave, and drop. They nodded. They are accomplices.

I lie down and close my eyes. I think I fall asleep.

When I wake the sun is falling toward the edge. Even the mosquitoes have tired. I stretch out and part the grass and look out at the haymakers. They see me and wave. They are inviting me over.

We hide behind the haystack and share black bread and bad vodka and talk with our hands about what Russians always talk about.

10

THE NEXT DAY and the next we rode on a strip of asphalt hung over the land like a bridge. Below us was bog. All around us bog. It was as if once there had been an ocean here but then time happened and filled it in with age and dirt and profanity.

We pedaled in a loose line, the front rider calling out whenever we were about to pass through a cloud of insects—you'd quick clop your mouth shut, hold your breath, pinch down your eyes and in seconds feel a sticky wave rush over you. On through, you would open your eyes and spit, chucking the bugs off your lips. If they had gone up your nose, you'd turn your head sideways, hold a thumb against one nostril, and snort.

Already Carl and his camera crew had found more interesting things to film. We saw them only at camp in the evening. And the press were also thinning out. And, although the cops and an occasional unmarked sharkmobile were still following us, they stayed out of sight. Tom and I had threatened to quit if they didn't back off. We could do that. The rumplesuits had made a mistake. By arranging banquets in each lost town we reached and allowing the Soviet press to ballyhoo about us—first Americans to see the secrets of Siberia and first to ride bicycles across the great fatherland and first to experience the fatherland's spanking new freedom, waxing on for columns—they had unintentionally empowered us. They were deathly

afraid we would fly back to America and tell lies about their
hospitality.

One day, west of Khabarovsk, when talk was as featureless as
the terrain and time pliable and sweat running down our back,
someone shouted: *"Vilosipedisty!"* Cyclists.

Astonished, we stopped immediately. Coming through the
haze were tiny patches of color. Orange and red and blue swaying and popping. Soon we could make out bumping shoulders
and bouncing legs. They were riding in a pack riding hard. In
moments they whirred up, enveloping us in a circle of razor
wheels, curious smiles and glistening young bodies.

The only man of any age, still straddling his bike, hopped
forward clicking his cleated feet on the pavement. We each
shook his hand. He was the coach. He had a pirate's mustache
and knotty thighs.

"The youth cycling club of Birobidzhan has come to welcome
you. To ride with you." He was very proud.

I looked around the circle. Girls and boys. Thirteen or fourteen, no older. Smooth damp faces, hairless and crimson as the
skin of a cherry. My eyes on their eyes and then their eyes
jumping anxiously away. I looked at their bodies. Lean, almost
angular, with slender muscles grafted to sinuous joints. It was
as if the substance and form of their bodies were the reincar-
nation of their machines. Tendons only spokes, blood only oil,
their lithe limbs like their tempered frames.

Without another word the youths spun their bikes around
and exploded away. Suddenly we were over thirty cyclists riding
close and quick over the marsh. Plaiting, in and out and back in.

The pace quickened so much the marsh smeared. Shoulder
to shoulder and knees and lungs and murmuring and sometimes a shout. I could taste the adrenaline. They could taste it.
They were young. They breathed it and it intoxicated them.
They willed to trounce and show and prove, to try hard as their
hard legs could try and ride how they imagined great cyclists
ride: hard until their hearts burst.

The pace spasmed again. The pack narrowed. Now we were
riding in pairs. Just you and your partner your brother your
blood and speed slurring the landscape.

I was to the right and just ahead of a boy with long flat feet spinning freckled knees. He had big ears sprouting from red hair. His head was down. He was concentrating, adroitly navigating his craft an inch from mine. I could see the blood surging through his temples and dried white spittle at the corners of his mouth. He was smiling outrageously.

From nowhere, a phantom cyclist sped past the boy and slid in just ahead of him. It was a swift, precise gesture. Their wheels almost touched.

The cyclist's body was so close to me: narrow back, a tight waist, cropped curly black hair, muscled hips set gracefully on the saddle, and legs, smooth long legs twirling lubricately. The head turned and dark eyes swung at me, challenged me, then snapped back up the road. I glanced over my shoulder at the redheaded boy. He looked desperate. I caught his face and grinned. He grinned back so I kicked the pedals, pulled forward, and looked left.

A girl. Everything around her was out of focus but she was clean and clear and right beside me. Her head down and hair in her face. Her small breasts, nipples like buttons, poking out from a flat chest.

She looked over at me, straight at me in the eyes, and smiled. Just a smile. There was nothing under her smile. Nothing behind it. She was that reckless age just a breath before that. The age before the fire of mendacity and ulterior motives and everlasting falling. The age when gender doesn't matter and a girl will still smile just a smile and laugh nothing more than a laugh and can beat a boy at most anything and hasn't given it a second thought.

She turned her head back. She looked through the top of her eyes down the road and pedaled hard. I pedaled harder to keep up. We were riding very fast. In seconds we spun around the rest of the pack and took the damp open pavement for ourselves.

I saw her legs again. Legs so long. A woman's legs strong and velvety hooked to a high, tight curved bottom. I saw she didn't know this. Her entire body was tight and smooth and she didn't know it. She was playful and glossy and just wanted to ride.

She had an aristocratic nose on a narrow face. Olive skin and dark eyebrows. She was half smiling. In any other world she would have been shy. But here, in *her* world, in her sexless, unfettered, unmuzzled world in the saddle, no. Here she was sure and unapologetic.

"How are you today?" She spoke in broken British without looking over.

"How are you?" I said. This made her drop her head, lift her eyebrows and smirk.

"Birobidzhan is twenty-seven kilometers from here," she said.

"You ride here often?"

"Yes. Now," she said. The air was touching her neck and combing her curls. She did not look at me. It was not necessary. We were side by side and so close we could feel the heat from each other. We were still moving faster and faster, thrumming inside.

"Now?" I said breathlessly.

"Now I have my own bicycle." She was curved over her craft, her small breasts pointing down, her fingers squeezing the handlebars.

"From my father. For my birthday."

I wanted to ask her more. I wanted to ask her how old she was and what grade she was in and if she had brothers and sisters and where her mother and father worked. I was struck. I wanted to ask her why she rode her bike the way she rode her bike even though I already knew and could remember and knew she would think the question so silly she would not bother to answer. I wanted to have her look at me so I could look at her but before I could say a word she stood up and thrust her body forward and we began speaking another language.

The drop of a little finger off the handlebars to warn of a piece of glass, the almost imperceptible nod to point out a pothole, the slight twisting of her head to show me something on the landscape, the steady breathing as if a chant or a song or psalm were inside us, and the delicate swerving to keep our bodies touching. She was arching her back, shifting her crotch on the saddle.

She moved one hand and changed gears so that we were pedaling at exactly the same cadence, our bodies moving in unison, legs going up and down and up and down. This delighted her and she laughed. Then she shifted up a gear and plunged forward a few inches. She was playing with me, teasing me. I shifted and rammed up to her. She pumped even harder. Now she was pushing and pulling and shoving, writhing her legs. Her face was red and her eyes were back and her head drifting back.

She was pumping. She was trying to leave me behind. Shaking and stretching and reaching. She tilted her head and wet curls washed across her face. She smiled again, her face strange, hard and soft. Now she wanted to ride with me. To pull me where she was going. She had no idea how fast she was going. She had no idea how fast she could go. She knew only how strong she was. How strong she imagined herself to be.

I was barely with her. I was being ridden, destroyed, my body aching, my chest swelling like bellows, mouth biting the air, sweat pouring off my chin.

Her face was flushed. We were in faultless harmony, air rushing around us as if we were one. Her legs squirming in frenzied circles, her arms pulling, her nipples erect and hard her mouth open her eyes half-shut her arms pulling and pulling legs jerking hips pumping when suddenly she looked at me and her eyes straightened and widened and her tongue fell back.

She slacked off. Our pace evened. Breathing and breathing and letting the bike move itself. Stroking and sliding and slipping but never speaking. She wanted it that way.

After we had partially recuperated, when she knew I was watching, she threw her head back and looked for a long moment down the road, as if she had lost something. I peered behind us. We were miles ahead of the pack. Ahead and alone.

When I turned around she was gone, bounding ten yards out in front, trilling, laughing, almost singing. I was behind, I could see her lunging feverishly, her back, her hips, her whole tight body humping the pedals. I stomped and stood up and stomped and caught her. I hung in. She weaved ferociously cutting diagonally across the road. I lost her. A peal of laughter flew back for me. I was breathing and burning and she was weaving back and forth and I could not catch her could never catch her never for she was young and wild and I was old and profane and fallen. I stabbed forward, caught her, lost her. She dove madly, left and then right leaning her bike dangerously and skillfully as if all there ever was all there ever could be was this flight and this chase. I lost her. I missed her. I came close. I lost and charged and lost again. Then she took a curve too wide and I lunged forward and drove in hard and she looked back and saw me trying to breathe and my face distorting, and she laughed again, and then smiled, and then stopped pedaling.

Speed and power and heat slowly drained from us. Now our heads were empty and wet, our arms and legs heavy. We were just gliding, fast but slowing, gliding through the haze. Her long, long legs were still. Her thighs were quivering. She was bent forward. She was breathing staring down through her handlebars, sweat dropping off the end of her nose, her mouth open with joy.

II

I GOT my second bike when I was eleven. It was black. Walking my paper route had become impossible.

I bought it brand-new, choosing it without hesitation from a dazzling row of stallions. I paid half. Dad chipped in the other half and bought the basket. That was one of the deals with Dad.

The basket was enormous. A wire crate deep and wide enough to hold fat Sunday papers or four sacks of groceries. My bike stood patiently in the driveway, shining and proud, while Dad and I mounted the basket in front of the handlebars. Steve watched solemnly with his fidgety hands in his trouser pockets that were my trouser pockets the summer before. I knew the basket obscured my steed's svelteness, but the paper route had paid for it and the paper route would pay for patches or a new tube when I ran over a nail.

I jumped on and careened down the block swerving and looping and yelling, feeling all over inside what I had lost six years before.

To me it was as if I were suddenly just like Clarissa Destin. She lived across the street. She was fifteen and got to drive a red car made in France. She always waved frantically and smiled with her eyes fuzzing and her lipstick just right as if it could cut you.

Actually, I knew I was far luckier. I could cut corners. I could

65

race sprinklers. I could zoom crosswalks where even a little car could never fit or ride out to the lake and dunk my front wheel into the mud and salamander water. I could again acrobat beneath the sanguine roses.

And now I could deliver papers, fast. If I overslept, which I always did, I could ride my whole route in a furious twenty-five minutes. Down the sidewalk through the morning dark, blindly reaching into the basket with one hand and just at the infallible moment, hurling the paper like a hand grenade. It would bounce once and roll right up to the door but by then I would be pitching the good news at another new house.

I rode my black big-basket bike every day for four years. But the paper route didn't last. Even with the bike I didn't like getting up so early and I didn't like collecting from cheap people. I quit and decided to mow more lawns but I never took off the basket. It held my books and gym bag when I got into junior high.

My junior high was a mile and a half away. A towering brick block erected in the middle of the prairie in 1889. On the walls in the gym were brown photos of muscling boys with arms folded. They looked tough, like boxers.

I never took the bus. This was back when Wyoming got snow all the time but I never took the bus because I loved bicycling in the snow. I yearned for it. It took skill. You could end up under the wheel of a car if you didn't have skill. I would make other Moms turn pale, too paralyzed to even honk as I skidded and slidded and danced balletlike by. Those were the Moms who wouldn't let their kids ride their bikes because they were afraid something might happen. Those were the Moms who had kids to whom nothing ever did.

I especially liked icy streets. Charging hard as I could then throwing the full force of my little body backward onto the brake. I'd spin in a full circle before falling slow as if I were really going to get hurt really going to crack my head wide open, then nonchalantly set out a foot. It was masterful.

I liked riding in blizzards even if I got frostbite on my earlobes. I would wear Mom's wool mittens, but on splintery days when the air was so cold it hurt your teeth, my hands would still freeze into claws that couldn't hold a pencil in first period.

My junior high had one thousand kids. There was only one bike rack. In the winter it was buried under snow and almost empty. Even in the windwicked fall and whipwindy spring there weren't that many bikes. I knew what that meant: The other kids were walking (slow and boring), getting a stuffy ride from Mom listening to news (fast but boring), or riding the bus (slow and boring and cold, and humiliating, because you had to wait on the corner in a line).

Me, I was autonomous. If I had to, and the streets were dry, I could make it to school in nine minutes. Spring out of bed spoon down hot cereal bound outdoors madly transport myself over the earth arriving pink and panting and exultant. On the infrequent occasions when I managed to rise early, I'd ride by parked cars kicking off the ice stalactites or blast through tumbleweeds behind the church or make a big loop through town exploring new streets.

The only other kids who were truly autonomous, like me, were the Mexicans. They lived over the viaduct across the railroad tracks. The bus didn't go there and their Moms didn't have cars so some kids would ride all year round, like me. The Mexicans they had bad bikes but they were good on them. They could fly up a curb popawheelie and land perfect. They could popawheelie in the middle of the street and pedal on the back wheel half a block and then when they felt like it just only when they felt like it set it down nice and easy and look over with the Itoldyousosucker smile. They deserved it. I could never do that. I enjoyed jumping my bike off the red dirt mounds in the prairie behind my house but I wasn't fancy. Once I screwed up and came down straddling the bar and lay there gasping and curled up with my face in the dust hoping no one saw. Tricks weren't my thing. I just liked to ride.

In summer I would ride all day. Ride right into night zipping through the streets. Me and the other bike-night kids we'd get bottle rockets from an old man in a shack out on the highway and howl back into town, divvy up, and have war blasting them at each other and tracing the night sky until someone would call the cops and we'd scatter like one of those rockets exploding sparks down dark alleys across backyards behind black houses but me I'd take off through the prairie and ditch behind high sagebrush under the white moon and lie low and the cops would go by rubbernecking and bullhorning and failing ignominiously. Then we'd regroup to rejoice at our stealth and courage.

One time I gave a girl a ride home from the baseball park. The baseball park was where the other kids hung out in the summer. I didn't go there much. I quit baseball because I was afraid to hit the ball. But I went there one calm blue evening and somehow met this girl.

We sat next to each other. I pretended to know baseball, clapping when everybody else clapped and making a half-hearted attempt at shouting at the ump. Mostly I stared at her. I couldn't help it.

We were in science together so we talked about how the teacher liked to wear tight shirts and flex his muscles when he wrote on the chalkboard. He tried to seduce the girls. She was beautiful and didn't wear lipstick. She said, "No, I think it's disgusting."

The sky went dark. The ballpark lights came on, hovering over the field like immense lightning bugs. It was a giddy warm summer night and we were sitting so close our legs touched and then the greatest thing happened. Her ride left. She didn't know it. She was supposed to get a ride home with somebody's sister but then we were somehow talking easy and fast about all kinds of things and had forgotten the ball game as if we were in a bubble all alone and when we looked up the game was over and her ride was gone.

I offered my humble services. I got anguished thinking she might think it was dumb but then I knew she didn't have any way home and would get in trouble if she was late so the whole thing was in my favor.

"I won't sit in that ugly thing."

I recovered quickly. "No, no. You sit on the seat, I'll pedal."

I thought my voice might have cracked but by now it was deep dark and the lightning bugs had been swatted out of a starry sky and I was her ride and she lived two splendorous miles away. My heart was reeling and chirping before I even pushed off. She almost slipped from the saddle and instead of screaming the way I thought she would she just laughed and steadied herself with her hands around my waist.

I flew through our dark town. I had amazing strength. Unknown endurance. I was galloping and breathing hard but trying to be quiet and stoic with sweat going down my back and her hands around my waist. I wanted to pedal like a falling star and fly her home quick in a blink to impress her but I wanted to pedal forever and slide and glide like a star falling so slow.

Then there was her street, and her house, and her front yard.

I dipped gracefully and she slid off. Her hands left my waist, squeezing once. I flexed my shoulders. She smiled. I smiled. She said thanks. Incredulous, I said thank *you*. We both were hot and itchy. The porch light burst on and she ran to the door and I jumped back in the saddle and pushed away and started pedaling, crazy with glory and triumph.

I glanced back. She was looking the other way stepping into her house and closing the door behind her but one hand was peeking around, waving.

Suddenly I heard a smash and zinging and felt shocked or punched and couldn't see or think and everything was rushing bleary dark bright and then knew I was in the air. Floating. Then dropping. Dropping so slow like when you want to say something but you don't know what so you don't say anything and your gut aches and I threw out my hands and maybe yelped and prepared to die and landed softly in six inches of hay in the bed of a parked pickup truck.

Seven years later we moved in together. Then I had to go explore my earth and she went to Australia and got married.

12

ONE HOT AFTERNOON we were waved off the road by a round woman.

"*Dobra pazhalavat. Zakhaditye, pasmatritye kakmy zhivyom,*" she shouted. Welcome! Come see how we live. We followed her into a village.

In the village there was a picnic waiting for us. Two card tables covered with an old tablecloth were set up in the dirt street. Two silver samovars filled with scalding Soviet coffee sat on top. The good china was out, a dozen blue-flowered cups on matching saucers. In a big blue bowl was fried bread stuffed with potatoes and rice.

There was fresh warm milk. A woman in a starched smock, her face dimpled as a baby's rear, dipped glass after glass from an enameled white pail. Woodback chairs were arranged beneath a wave of purple lilac bushes.

A tractor groaned around a corner flinging dried mud. The houses were small and set back from the street. A little girl chattered a stick along a fence. A dog. Not a cloud.

This was a cooperative farm.

It was the manager of the co-op who had hailed us down. She was big as a barrel with a tanned face and white hair. She pulled us over to the card tables, gave us plates, made us load them till

71

they were spilling over, then guided us into the shade of the lilacs.

Torie began asking questions and Tanya translated.

The manager said there were 1,307 residents of the co-op. Each family lived in a brick single-story duplex on a large plot of land. Each family had at least one milk cow, several pigs, a goat and a garden. The co-op itself was primarily a dairy farm, machine-milking eight hundred cows but also running four hundred head of beef cattle. The community had its own school and clubhouse. A council made local decisions. The chairman of the council was also the manager of the co-op.

The manager spoke briskly, as though she had said it all a hundred times before. I interrupted and asked about production quotas.

"Moskva," she said, rolling her eyes. "They are set in Moscow, it is ridiculous. Moscow is thousands of kilometers away. They have no idea what's going on out here." She waited for my next question. I was too slow. She moved on. I liked her.

The co-op sold its milk and beef to the state, which then distributed it to the state-run groceries. Whatever was left after the quota was met, they could sell at local markets and keep the profits.

"We always produce more than the quota," she said.

"Who takes care of the children?" Torie asked.

"All women get two years' paid maternity leave, then they must go back to work. We have a good day care, although we need a new building. That is a problem."

She went on to say that the school needed more books and the crop-rotation system needed modifying and that personal automobiles were obtained through seniority—when your name reached the top of the list, you could buy a car.

"If you have the money. Wages here are above average, workers get a hundred-fifty to three hundred rubles a month, but a car costs nine thousand."

We had finished eating now. Tom was oiling the chain on his bicycle and listening from a distance. Fyodor, Pavel and Natasha were acting bored—the brothers pulling on their beards and gazing nowhere, Natasha picking a scab on her elbow. Suddenly Fyodor snatched up his bicycle and rode off.

Pavel and Natasha wheeled after him. The woman paid no attention.

"Enough numbers. I know what you want. You want to see how we live." She was looking at Torie and me. She hooked her arms through our elbows, caught Tanya with one hand and strolled us across the street. We walked through a gate into an immense green garden and on up to a brick house.

"This is my home. In Russia, the home is all that matters. It is our sanctuary." She opened the front door and gently pushed us in.

A hallway divided the house in half. On the right were three small bedrooms, each spare and tidy as a child ready for church. At the end of the hall was a stone hearth. It burned wood and coal and heated the house. On the left side of the hall was the living room and kitchen. The walls in the living room had Persian rugs. There were two sofas and a TV. In the kitchen was a wood stove, a plastic counter, and crooked yet exasperatingly neat cupboards. The kitchen had cold running water. The facilities were in the backyard.

We poked around and kept asking questions.

Were all the homes in the co-op like this?

She grinned. "Well, everyone decorates differently, but, in general, yes."

Did the TV work?

"As well as any TV in Siberia. The two government channels," she said. "I saw *you* on TV. That's how I knew you would be coming."

Did she like her work?

She tilted her bulky head and surveyed her home. "Yes. Yes I like it very much. My life here, my family, it is good. . . ."

She paused. "You know that you are going so slow through my country. You are going to see many bad things. When you see them, remember my home."

She escorted us outside and around to the backyard. The backyard was also a green garden. We walked down a path to a shed. She showed us several pigs and warned us about slipping on the manure.

On our way back through the garden she began naming the vegetables she'd planted and the kinds of flowers she'd laced through her fence. As we passed beside the house, I stopped to look inside one last time.

I was looking into a bedroom. Bare walls, a small dresser, a heavy red rug. I spotted something on the bed and drew closer, shading the glass with my hands.

On the quilt was a very round Matrioshka doll—they are carved from a solid piece of wood. It was simply painted with bright colors, red and blue and green. The top half of the doll was lying beside its body, revealing the smiling face of the next doll inside.

Less than an hour after leaving the farm co-op, we were again waved off the road. This time by rumplesuits standing beside their sharkmobiles. We were escorted into a tenement town. We were told to put our bicycles in a truck garage. We were told to board a bus. The bus took us to a café.

Not a public café. There were fans on the ceiling and real flowers in crystal vases. Several large portraits of Him hung on the walls. There were a dozen waitresses. They smiled profusely. They wore tremendous makeup and ruffled outfits that showed something at both ends when they bent over. There were bottles of imported liquor across the mahogany bar beneath an enormous beveled mirror.

We were seated and given linen napkins and cool glasses of water. The doors were locked behind us and the speeches began.

"We are a proud people proud to welcome you brave bicycling soldiers to our proud but humble city . . ."

and the waitresses began loading the tables. First the hors d'oeuvres: caviar, two black varieties and one red, a selection of specialty sardines, deviled eggs made to look like little boats, and an extravagant display of pickled carrots and cauliflower. Next, lettuce-laced bowls of scallops and shrimp. Then brilliant vegetable casseroles. Our choice of drinks—milk or wine or Cuban coffee or tea or fruit juice or Chinese beer or bottled water or carbonated beverages. Then the tureens of soup and sliced white bread and big sweet rolls and fish dishes and meat dishes and three kinds of dessert

". . . and, great American comrades, our industrious people are so because they are all equal, happy, free and fulfilled."

I tried to ask a question. Questions were prohibited.

Torie, Tom and I, and Tanya, were still full from the lunch at the co-op. We couldn't eat. We were eyeballed and considered rude guests. Fyodor ate. Pavel and Natasha made a good show of eating and watched the speechmakers to see how they did it.

Then we paid. We had paid for every rumplesuit banquet since entering the Soviet Union. We had attended over two dozen. "This is the way Soviets do things," said Tanya.

That night in camp we told Carl we would henceforth avoid all banquets. Carl laughed. He had already lined up a camp cook.

Her name was Leah. She reminded me of the director of the co-op, except Leah was even rounder, round as a milk cow, and happier. She rode in the supply truck, her great weight bumping, a heavy pink arm hanging in the sun and waving enthusiastically when we bicycled by.

Ordinarily Leah was a cook on one of the Trans-Siberian trains. She was used to cooking for a crowd, used to finding food in villages with empty grocery stores. She made silk purses from sows' ears regularly.

She cooked cabbage stew cabbage soup cabbage salad cabbage sandwiches coleslaw, boiled potatoes fried potatoes scalloped potatoes mashed potatoes potato soup, and the same with tomatoes and cucumbers. Goulash a hundred ways. And all of it, even breakfast, with scoops of hard white lard and gallons of fresh milk.

The first night on the job she built and then slaved over a large campfire. She fed us, the cyclists, first. Then the driver of the supply truck. Then the film crew. Then, reluctantly, the cops and rumplesuits who dropped in. She ate last.

Later that night Tanya and I went for a walk.

"Leah is Russian," she said.

I nodded.

"No. Leah is *Russian*, not Soviet."

The second day Leah forced the rumplesuits to buy her a gas range and a tank of gas. I saw her standing beside a sharkmobile poking her thick finger into one of the doughy suits.

The stove and tank sat in the back of the supply truck. The

bed of the truck was chest high. That evening, when the truck driver had strayed off into a village pursuing a woman in a purple dress, Leah lifted the range down herself. And the tank. She hooked them up and began fixing dinner and when we came dogging into camp, there she was, standing merrily before her gas range, her cotton dress rummied from hauling a burlap sack of onions, wide sweat stains under her arms, wool slippers squashed flat in the muddy birch leaves.

The third evening I lifted the lid of a pot and got scalded and she slapped me with her paws and laughed and yelled at me and placed a heavy knife and two loaves of bread in my hands. I sliced the bread. After dinner she piled the aluminum dishes into a pail, handed the bucket to me, put her arm through mine and walked us into the woods. We did dishes in a creek, without soap, using sand to scrub the grease from the plates.

The next night she had me cut the bread again and open a few cans. She asked Tanya to slice the block of butter. We had boiled potatoes and vegetable goulash for dinner. Afterward, when everyone else had scuttled into their tents, Leah and I walked down to a lake to do dishes.

It was a still, cool evening. We walked right into the water. By the time we finished the dishes the sun had dropped into the trees. The lake had turned dark blue. The stars were coming out. Leah bent up slowly, her huge hard body groaning, her stubtoe feet grinding on the rocks in the cold water. She looked at the trees and the sky and the water, and whispered, *"Moy synochik, eta Sibir."* My little son, this is Siberia.

From that night on, Leah called me her *synochik,* her little son. She had a real son somewhere in Siberia, but he was grown and gone.

Sometimes out of nowhere Leah would hug one of us the way Russian people hug, with both arms, squeezing hard. She spoke to us in Russian. She never thought we didn't understand because we always did. Leah spoke the old language, the language of the country before 1917. If she needed something, she needed that very something. If it was a big thing, she needed the big thing, if small, then small. If Leah felt something, she felt that very thing.

"Leah doesn't speak Soviet," Tanya said one morning, "So-viet is what they speak." She pointed to the rumplesuits.

Leah liked me and Tanya to help her. Mostly little things she thought we could do right—peeling potatoes cutting cucumbers fetching water. The hard stuff or the heavy stuff she did herself because she knew she was the Russian babushka.

Leah liked to sing while she cooked. She would stand in front of her makeshift stove in the woods and sing. Not loud, the way you would think for a woman of such size, but soft and high as a small girl.

Leah liked to have a smoke after dinner. A little stub in her mouth that the truck driver might have given her. She would squat on a stool and put her great arms straight out on her knees. Her body would completely hide the stool. She would play, pull the cigarette away in plump fingers and blow smoke through pouty lips and throw out her arm trying to smoke sophisticated and then laugh wonderfully and flash her heavy blue eyes as if she were actually a sheer young thing caught inside some old working woman's body. After her smoke she would hold Felix on her forearm and stroke him.

One day it was the Fourth of July. She knew this day. She fixed a large meal, even larger than usual, and made a special dessert with strawberries. At dinner, in the mucky woods, she wore lipstick and mascara and blush on her cheeks even though she didn't need it because her wide face was always so red from cooking. She would have looked comical if you didn't know she was trying to look beautiful, and did look beautiful.

After dinner she told me to get the Cuban coffee out of the back of the truck. I laughed. I thought she was joking with me.

"*Prinositye Kuba kofye,*" she said again.

I crawled up into the supply truck and found a case of Cuban coffee.

There were twenty tins inside the box. She popped one open and dumped the whole thing into a pot. She took a long time boiling it. It was cowboy coffee, grounds and all. She made me scrub the aluminum cups and hand them out. When it was ready and just perfect and she had tested it with a spoon as if

it were soup, she walked around camp in the dark and poured
each person a full cup. The act alone delighted her. And the
coffee, the coffee was rich and robust. I had no idea how she
had procured it.

"Wonderful coffee Leah," said one of the rumplesuits. He
was almost invisible sitting in his sharkmobile under the pine
trees in the dark.

Later that night she showed off the empty tin, passing it
around. I knew she was going to save it. Find a place for it on
a shelf in her house that was only a cabin in some Siberian town
with hardly a name.

The next morning she was up before all of us standing
over her gas range in the trees in the striping yellow light.
She was always up before all of us. I tried to imagine her lum-
bering on her hands and knees, emerging like a bear from
her small tent.

When I got up she told me to get the coffee out of the truck.
I crawled in over the burlap sacks and searched for the box. It
was gone.

"*Kofye, nyet?*" said Leah flatly.

"*Da,*" I said. She balled one huge pink hand into another.

"*Kofye, nyet?*" she repeated, her voice low.

I nodded.

Her jowls flinched. "*Prinasitye chay.*"

We had tea with breakfast. Someone asked where the coffee
was. Leah said there was no coffee and kept stirring her pot on
her stove in the wet woods.

One of the rumplesuits shouted from his vehicle, "Aaaah,
this is such good *chay.*"

Someone said again, "Where is the Cuban coffee?"

The same suit started to laugh as such men all over the world
laugh. "You are in Siberia American cyclist. Cuba is far away?"
He laughed again.

"The coffee we had last night."

"We did not have coffee last night."

Natasha and Fyodor and Pavel were sitting together around
a campfire. They didn't raise an eye.

"The coffee we had last night."

"We did not have coffee last night. We have never had coffee, always this wonderful *chay* that Leah makes." The rumple-

suit looked over at Leah and smiled and raised his cup of tea. Leah turned her back.

Shouting broke out. We were all shouting. We were naive Americans. The Soviets did not say a word. Not even Tanya.

At lunch, we had coffee again. Leah smiled to herself and hugged me. She had used up her own salary to get it. It was scalding Soviet coffee.

13

WE REACHED the sealed city of Blagoveshchensk that same day. Sharkmobiles surrounded us on the outskirts of town. We were ceremoniously welcomed. A pretty woman in sequined slippers and a scarlet costume stood in the road and proffered white bread and salt. She smiled fixedly. It was the traditional Russian greeting for great travelers. There were tumid speeches. We would be on TV and in the newspaper. We were taken to a big hotel.

Blagoveshchensk is a remote city. The region west and north of Blagoveshchensk is entirely missing from *The Official Road Atlas of the Soviet Union,* as if those pages had been torn out—as if someone had found something out there he didn't want to share. In world atlases, a thin red line runs into this no-man's-land, turns to dashes, and then disappears for a thousand miles. Only the black thread of the Trans-Siberian Railroad, with its knots of unknown settlements—Ushumum, Tygda, Magdagachi, Dzhalinda—crosses the emptiness to the city of Chita.

When we got to our hotel, there was a letter waiting for me. I slipped it into my pocket and slunk out into the street.

Blagoveshchensk lies where the Zeya River flows into the mighty Amur, the northern border between China and Russia. There is a concrete walkway along the Amur. I walked beside the wide brown river watching the barges. They were moving slowly, so slowly it seemed as if they were mired in the water. After dark, I bought a bottle of good vodka and returned to my room. I poured a tall glass, sat on the floor and held the letter.

The letter was from Sue. Sue. The one I left to come here. Sue my unseen side. Just sitting on the floor in the dark, holding the letter, I could feel her.

After a while I opened the letter. I read it. I drank the vodka. I was reading the words and they were of course just normal words saying nothing at all like all love-letter words

> . . . and when you get back, your jeans will still be hanging on the bedroom door and your cowboy boots will still be in the closet, and I will be here.

but they carried me to her. To her tongue. And her breasts. And the way she looked from the back and cowboy dancing and lying in the sagebrush and mornings when the snow was so deep we'd just listen to the radio on top of each other and here I was in some cement hotel on the edge of emptiness thinking, You're a fucking fool Mark.

Then I folded the letter and placed it in the back of my journal and made a promise not to read it again because you can't let your head go back home like that. At least not at the beginning of a trip. It's like letting a salmon go. A hot thick-bodied salmon. All it'll do is plunge back upstream, no matter how far away you are no matter how powerful the current is, and you'll never finish your journey.

I stood up, wobbled a bit, and went down to the restaurant.

The restaurant was large, more like a dance hall. It was smoky and loud and crowded. Everyone was getting drunk and having fun. I found our table. The Soviets had already gone to bed.

I sat down and Tom handed me a glass of vodka. He pointed his chin toward an inconspicuous balcony. The rumplesuits were up there. They were watching us. I waved.

Torie and Tanya laughed. Then Torie looked at me. She knew. She'd gotten a letter from her girlfriend.

"How was the letter?"

I nodded.

She leaned over and touched my hand.

It was a humid night and the band was terrible. The band was screeching. They were doing it on purpose. We watched people dance and drink. The band played the exact same song seven times in a row. We drank until we couldn't hear it, then started dancing.

A young man stumbled to our table. He had heard us speaking English. He was so happy he started to cry. He had taught himself English. Alcohol had turned his tongue to mush but he still spoke well. He grabbed me by the shoulders and banged his square head against mine and shouted that his greatest dream was to go to America. He was momentarily wild with excitement. He was spraying his words. And now Americans were here in his city and he was talking to them. *Bozhe moy,* he said. My God. He wanted to write us so we put our addresses on a napkin. He was crying watching us write down our addresses. He folded the napkin concentrating very hard and placed it in his breast pocket. Then he shouted that he would now write his address so we could write him. He bent over a wet napkin. Vodka had spilled on the napkin.

A girl from the table behind us, a table crowded with girls, dragged him back. She said excuse him. I said no problem. She asked me to dance. We danced. We were the same height, her cheeks were hot. She pressed them against mine. Her name was Savka. Her dress clung damply to her body so I could see her breasts and her flat stomach. She had big young eyes searching me. She held me so tight we moved slow. The song ended and the same song began again and we kept dancing. I asked her why the band played the same song over and over.

Balota, she said.

I shook my head.

She held me very tight and we kept dancing. She whispered in my ear.

When you are suffering you want other people to suffer.

We danced so close I could feel her ribs. She asked me if I was staying in this hotel. I said yes before thinking. She asked to sleep with me. She kissed me on the neck. She moved her hips. The girls from her table were watching us. We danced to the same song again.

I got out of it by giving her my address. She was happy, as if that was all she really wanted.

Then it was ten-thirty. The band stopped. Savka and her brother and all the girls at the table had vanished. The rumplesuits descended from the balcony.

"Tomorrow you will board the train for Chita."

"Dear miscreants . . ." Tom spoke softly. He was drunk and more serious than I had ever seen him. "We will not take the train."

"There is no road. You cannot go where there is no road."

"We must."

"It is impossible."

"Then most definitely we must."

In the morning we bicycled west away from Blagoveshchensk. The road began dwindling at once. By evening the pavement was gone.

The next day the gravel turned to mud and the land closed in. Swamp and forest everywhere. Mud everywhere.

At the end of the day an unknown sharkmobile fishtailed down the road to catch us. It stopped beside Fyodor. A piece of paper came out the window. It was a telex from Moscow, the blessing of the rumplesuits. It didn't say we could not ride where there was no road. It didn't say we could. It didn't say there was no road. It said they were not responsible if we pedaled into Siberia and never came back out and they were if we made it and were heroes.

That day the supply truck had gotten stuck in the mud three times. The film-crew jeep twice. They would have to turn back. Back to Blagoveshchensk to be put on a flatbed and trained around the hump of Manchuria to the city of Chita. At dark, Carl called a camp meeting.

"So you have what you want," he said.

"Yes," said Tom. "We do. Do you?"

"Not yet."

I was trying to understand what Carl meant, when it all came clear. Carl was leaving us. He was saying good-bye. He was the first Western filmmaker to be here and he knew it. He wanted to film Siberia.

We would hardly see Carl and his film crew again.

*   *   *

I helped Leah that night for the last time.

We were camped in small pines beside a muddy river. Leah made a massive farewell meal. At dinner, after drinking liquor that Leah had procured, Tanya gave her Felix. It was a present. Leah cried, her huge face creasing and turning red.

Then rain came and thundered in the forest sending everyone but Leah to their tents. In twenty minutes the storm passed on leaving the trees dripping and murmuring in slanted purple light.

I helped Leah clean up. She had worked right through the rain. I was dragging a sack of potatoes toward the truck when I heard her coming.

Then I was up in the air, floating, levitating beneath the pines.

She had swung one arm under my knees and one around my back, tipped me backward, and lifted me effortlessly off the ground. She twirled in the forest holding me straight out in her arms, laughing.

"*Moy synochik, zaftra ty payedish' v mayu stranu.*"

Tomorrow you go into my country.

PART TWO

14

A T DAWN we left. Seven cyclists riding single file through the blue forest. I had that grandness in me again.

The road wiggled through the woods. It wasn't even a road really, just a track of mud a foot deep, ruts brimming with fluid. Riding was treacherous and glutinous and wondrous. It took technique, concentration. Trick was to roll on the ridges between the ruts. They were narrow and slippery so you had to hit them dead on skimming straight across like an acrobat on a high wire. If you slowed down or let show any halfscared herkyjerky, let your handlebars torque or your legs hitch or worst of all lost faith thinking even for a flash you might fall, you did, off and down flailing in ooze black as tar up to your belly. So it was good bicycling, better than any since I was five.

We lost each other riding in the forest and only regrouped hours later when the trees spread back and the road reached a village.

Tanya asked a boy throwing rocks at a frog if the village had a *stalovaya*. A *stalovaya* was a "worker's cafeteria." The boy caught his frog, put it in his pocket and led us over the railroad tracks to a concrete building.

This *stalovaya* was also the school cafeteria. You had to duck your head to get in. The blue cement ceiling was so low and the bent cement walls so thick it felt as if you were inside a submarine. There were clean curtains in front of fogged windows and flowers in the deep window ledges and a sea of mud outside.

We dropped in looking as if we'd been dipped in dark chocolate, but the cooks didn't mind. They were big sweating women with ridiculous chef's hats. They pulled us into the kitchen and let us wash up at a pipe sticking out of the wall. It was the only water for the cafeteria. Then they sat us on low benches beneath long tables and fed us until we couldn't move. Vegetable soup fried liver fried potatoes hot bread hot chocolate. They watched us eat. They were big square women and liked to see such appetites. They didn't ask any questions. When we told them what we were doing they smiled. They smiled the smiles they must have used for precocious schoolchildren who told them they were going to grow up and go away from here. They didn't believe we had come on bicycles to their lost village. They didn't go outside to check.

After lunch we rode through the village. A young girl flew out from a fence gate. She was high on a high horse bike. She sidled up to me and we rode together beside the log cabins.

This little girl and I, we were riding above the mud through the village when her babushka shouted. The little girl twirled back around and threw her look to me and the babushka pointed past us into Siberia and shouted *Balota!* and the road stopped right at the last log cabin.

We saw it coming and no one spoke and we kept riding. We were ignorant. We still believed hesitation was weakness. We charged in like light cavalry and made it less than ten yards before the mud cut us down. It globbed onto our tires and rolled up under our fenders and our wheels stopped and we fell over and I was thinking of the cooks in the *stalovaya*.

I could see their smiles. They were smiling because we were hungry and eating right there in front of them and they had made a good meal for us and that was enough. And because they knew they lived in a Russian mud village with a mud road going in and no road going out. And maybe because they sometimes got electricity to their homes and could watch TV and see something of the world outside, soccer or Moscow or soldiers or famous people like cosmonauts, and so understood in a very ordinary way that they lived in the largest country on the planet and that it was a country that could have cosmonauts and tanks but couldn't put a road across itself.

Our bikes lay in the mud like shot horses. Tom and I got out our tools and we all stripped off our fenders.

I looked behind me and saw the little girl. She was standing beside her bicycle. It was as tall as she was. She was waving. I waved back, then turned and looked west.

Far as the eye could see, mud. Mud smooth and black as oil. An ocean of mud with trees and grass growing in it.

We stood our steeds up and started trotting forward pushing our bikes. Mud clodded onto our feet and hucked in our faces and we kept running and pushing and pushing and then one by one leapt on and rode glopping and slucking through earth soft as black butter soft as feces rotting the trunks off the trees drowning the yellow grass breeding insects sucking onto your face until you were choking.

Once I saw Fyodor behind me. He'd fallen and his bike was sunk on its side. Mud in his beard and hair and covering half his face as if he'd barely caught himself from going under. I was close to him but there was grass between us and he couldn't see me. His eyes were glaring across the swamp. He was in mud up to his balls. Bugs were swarming on him. He was standing very still. He slowly thrust his arms in the air and I could see the blood in his neck and the muscles around his chest and he screamed.

"SIBIRRRR!"

It was the first time I saw Fyodor smile.

We each went alone through the swamp for hours doing whatever we had to do to keep moving.

Then the land began foundering and the reeds and thatch rose up to our necks and we began sinking and then saw the railroad far off and set out thrashing and splashing dragging the bikes sideways and it seemed like hours and hours but then we were there lurching up the embankment. We fell down on the rocks and couldn't speak and couldn't think we were breathing so hard staring at nothing sitting on the rail with our eyes burning and the bugs eating our sweat and our bikes thrown down on the tracks trying to think just think think and thought Jesus we were arrogant Jesus we were insolent swaggering bastards fuck we made one huge mistake.

Then a train came. We sprang off the rails and slid our bikes down the slope and stood just above the water and grass while the rails clacked and boxcars clanked and the shadows chattered over us.

When the train passed we got our bikes back up between the rails and started walking.

We walked for the rest of the day. Our bikes hopping awkwardly on the ties and our faces cooking. Creosote burning our calves and spikes stubbing our swamp-soft toes.

Just before dusk when the air was rich and we were still above it all walking like hobos casting stretched moving shadows, we came to someplace. Four cabins clumped next to the tracks.

They appeared deserted. Then a man came out and looked at us. Then he turned and walked back inside the cabin. Fyodor and I dropped our bikes and ran after him. Fyodor knocked on the cabin door.

"*Zdrastvutye*," Fyodor yelled.

"Hello," I yelled.

"*My khatim pakupat' pisha*."

"We would like to buy food."

A woman in a wool sweater came out of the door. She walked around us on the planks laid in the mud to another cabin. She found the key in her apron and opened a lock the size of a horseshoe and went inside.

It was the general store. One room with a closet and a wood stove. We bought what we could. Wrapped candies she measured out on an ancient scale and two jars of fermented tomatoes and some packages of dry soup. She could tell we were disappointed. She stepped back into the closet and came out with a jar of milk.

Beyond the store in a tiny hayfield beside the tracks, the tents were already set up and Pavel had a fire going. The sky was bloody now and about to fall over. It happened quick and then the fire felt warmer and we huddled around until the soup was ready.

Two ragged boys each with his own dog came out of the dark to our fire. They were very happy to see us. They brought us a jar of honey and two loaves of dark bread—gifts from the store woman.

The boys got a kick out of their dogs trying to get the soup out of our bowls. They chased their dogs around in the dark and wrestled with them and then came back and asked us a lot of questions. As soon as they learned we really did come on bicycles they immediately found one and lifted it up by the handlebars and showed it to us like a trophy.

Then the man we had first seen appeared. He wasn't smiling. I thought for a moment he didn't like us putting a campfire in his hayfield, but he was drunk. He twitched his eyes looking at the fire. His suit coat and pants were greasy. Fyodor asked him questions but he didn't answer. One of the boys' dogs came close and he bent forward and reached his long slick hands out and got it and threw it into the dark.

The dog yelped and the boys came back from the blackness into the firelight. They walked right past him even though they seemed to know he might cuff them. They weren't scared. They patted their dogs.

Then we heard a deep rumbling. It was far away at first, but grew. The man stood up and walked onto the railroad tracks. The rumbling began to fill the night. The train was coming fast. The man stood on the tracks with his hands up in the air. Orange firelight licked along the rails. The man was dark up on the tracks, silhouetted, but when he turned his head, the firelight was in his eyes.

The boys did not look up at him. They tussled with their dogs.

The man had his hands up in the air and his head turned looking at us and now we could feel the earth starting to tremble and a log dropped in the fire sending up sparks and the man was still looking at us as if he had something to prove and would just as soon be cut in half by a train as come back and sit by the fire and then the train was right there flying howling thundering and we thought he would die, but at the last possible moment he dove off the far side of the tracks.

When the train had passed and the noise was distant, one of the boys, the precocious one with curly blond hair and grease from our bicycles on his face, resumed his questioning.

"Do boys have bicycles in America?" I told him some did.

"Did you have a bicycle when you were like me?" He pointed his grimy finger at me and then back at himself. I told him I did.

"Did you see any tigers yet?" I told him I hadn't and he said they were all around and looked out into the dark as if he wanted to go looking for one that very minute. He said he had seen tracks.

After he'd asked everything he could think of and listened intently to the answers, sitting on his haunches thinking it over looking at his friend through the fire and poking the fire with a stick and smiling, he said,

"When I grow up I'm going to get a bicycle and go away."

15

I HEARD the ax whacking, echoing, and shimmied out of my
bag. It was a cool morning, the kind that makes you feel lively
and young inside no matter where you are. I walked through
the dew to the campfire. It was out. Pavel was standing beside
a pile of birch saplings. He was delimbing them, then chopping
the poles into four-foot lengths. I didn't know what he was
doing and he didn't tell me.

I worked on the fire. Pavel took a walk along the railroad
tracks. He returned with a bundle of greasy wires. I gave him
a cup of tea and a honey sandwich.

"*Kleshi*," said Pavel.

I went to my tent to get the pliers from the repair kit. When
I returned Pavel was back on the railroad tracks. His bike was
lying between the rails. He had three lengths of birch under his
arm, the wires in one hand and the ax in the other. He called
me up onto the tracks.

Although the sun was out now the air was still brisk. Steam
was wafting off the tents. Standing between the rails, you could
see down the tracks in both directions forever. It was a beautiful
pink morning in the swamp. Only Pavel and I and the cuckoo
birds were awake.

Pavel asked me to balance his bicycle on one rail. I lifted it up
and steadied the wheels on the steel. Pavel took one of the

four-foot staves and held it alongside the front wheel next to the fork. The stave extended from the handlebars, down along the fork, past the tire and touching the side of the rail. It was apparently too long. He hacked off a section and held it up again. It seemed to suit him so he cut a second stave the same length.

He took the wires and the pliers and tightly fastened a stave to both sides of the front wheel along the fork. It looked like a splint. He wired the top ends of both staves to the handlebars; the bottom ends stuck down past the front tire along either side of the rail, in effect locking the front wheel onto the track. Pavel laid his head on the steel to check it.

Then he took the third stave and placed it along the top of the bicycle. It extended from under the saddle up to the middle of the handlebars. He wired it in this position so the handlebars could not turn.

"*Otpuskay*," Pavel said. Let go.

He took hold of the seat with just one hand and lightly pushed the bicycle forward. It balanced almost by itself and rolled quietly over the rail.

As everyone got up I sloshed into the birch and cut enough saplings for the rest of the staves. Pavel lopped them into the proper lengths and then shouted everybody onto the tracks to find their own wire.

After breakfast, under Pavel's supervision, we all fitted our bicycles with the sapling splints. We called it the "railroad rudder."

I don't know where the two boys were or their dogs or the man but we left without saying good-bye, in a long line on one rail, our bicycles newly retrofitted for the Trans-Siberian Railroad.

The day before, slogging through the gumbo beyond the last village, we'd made 2.8 miles in three hours (we knew because of our maddeningly waterproof odometers). Later, after abandoning the swamp to walk the rails—our bicycles bumping clumsily on the ties—we'd moved at about two miles an hour. Now, with the wheels in line rolling unimpaired on the rail, we were clipping along at a fantastic three miles per hour.

*   *   *

When I first met Pavel he said he had already bicycled across the Soviet Union. He said he was the first.

His brother Fyodor had said our bike ride was his twenty-fifth expedition. He said all of them had been complete successes.

Both Pavel and Fyodor are Soviets. They speak Soviet.

After a week Fyodor admitted that some of his expeditions had not been successes. They'd not always reached the summit or finished or done what they said they would do. Sometimes people had died.

In Blagoveshchensk, Tom and I had questioned Pavel about maps and routes and how we could best get through the imminent emptiness. Pavel hadn't answered. He wouldn't answer. We finally found out that Pavel Konyukhov, on his ride across the Soviet Union on a one-speed with a backpack, had taken the train through the swamp.

16

Once upon a time we were bicycling across the largest country on earth. Now we were walking, pushing our bicycles.

Pushing a bicycle is absurd. It is a sacrilege. Like pushing an airplane or rowing a sailboat. But when you're there, walking above the swamp with the rails skimming out in front of you, you're just so damn grateful not to be down there drowning in mud, you can't think about it. You don't think about it. Siberia is too big. Big as an ocean. Big as the sky. If you really let yourself think about it, it would gut you.

So you just walk. Walk and walk and walk and work on your rhythm and wait for grace. *Grace.* Grace only comes with rhythm and only grace will let you forget to think. So you push and push and wait and wait and step and step and step until a rhythm comes to you and some kind of magical blur and your mind starts doing funny things. Playing tricks the way it does right before you fall asleep. You'll be walking walketing walkatawalkata wlick wlack clickityclack like this and after a while grace will finally come for you and cut your head off like a sword cutting the string on a kite. Then your legs will be going along just fine and the bike moving smoothly atop the rail but you, you'll be gone.

Gone back to watching home movies. Running them in whatever order, slower in some parts where the color and the sound

99

and the story are better than they ever were. You're watching so close you fall in because when you're somewhere where you don't know where you are, someplace so edgeless and immense it makes you seasick, you go back to where you're sure you were and become exactly what you were there. You know that place and that ground and that person.

Fyodor went back to the North Pole. I knew because during lunch on the side of the tracks when I was skipping stones over green water, he would draw me pictures of his routes in the mud with a stick. He'd been to the North Pole three times. The world record would be four. That was next summer's expedition. After that he planned to sail around the world solo. He would have to make the trip four times because that record was also three. He guessed it would take him seven years.

I learned from Tanya that Natasha had a three-month-old baby so maybe she rocked her baby all day on the tracks above the swamp but I don't think so. I don't know. Tanya said Natasha came on the trip to get away from her baby because it cried too much. Natasha and Tanya shared a tent and hated each other so you had to think about it. I think Natasha spent the days sleeping with her boyfriends.

I didn't know where Pavel went. I didn't know anything at all about Pavel. I never would. Any talking he did Fyodor did for him.

I knew where Torie went. She went to Vermont. She said the land there cradled you because the mountains were close in and the sky warm pewter. She said she missed it. She said:

"You get a certain kind of brain from those kinds of mountains, intricate and historical and cultivated but not necessarily wide open."

Uh-huh I said.

"On the other hand, you Mark, you got a different kind of brain because you grew up in wide mountains above the plains. Those mountains made you not so historical or cultivated but open and not needing to be cradled."

I nodded.

"Wyoming is like that. I can see it all over in you."

Uh-huh.

When Torie talked about the brain she meant the heart. Of

course we never actually had this conversation it was just what she said to me.

Tanya spent most of her time in L.A. America. She'd visited a friend there for three weeks and had wanted to defect right then. But before she left Moscow the rumplesuits had talked with her. They had invited her to one of their windowless castle offices and told her if she didn't come back, her brother, who was an impassioned physicist, a rising-star scientist, would lose his job.

Tanya's mother, who Tanya said was very Jewish and weepy and addled and never hugged her during all her trying to grow up and hadn't even raised her—an aunt had raised her—told Tanya she would disown her if she did anything to jeopardize her brother's career. So Tanya came back to Moscow. But from then on she went to L.A. all the time.

Tom sometimes went back to Massachusetts, or Germany where he studied for a year, or Chicago where he went to a private school once, but usually it was Seattle. That's where his friends were. That's where he lived in a converted corner grocery store although he never stayed long. Soon enough he'd be back out to sea. Always back out to sea.

"I guess that's where I learned who I am," he said.

Yes I said.

"There's this time in a certain place you can remember down to the color of the air that you figure out who you are."

Uh-huh.

"Everybody seems to think it's some time when you're young but it's not. When you're young you're too sure of who you are to even come close to learning who you are."

But then it didn't matter where you went or how you got there as long as you kept walking and kept yourself sane. That was the deal. When you are alone you can go anywhere and let yourself go crazy if you feel like it. But traveling with other people, it's up to you to keep yourself sane. You're in a family and it's tough enough already.

Me, I went all over the world, but mostly back to Wyoming. I kept remembering a hobo I met once on a hot prairie day.

He dropped out of a boxcar and walked into town. He was wearing two pairs of pants and two shirts with both collars buttoned and the whiskery skin on his neck folding over and his hair scattered. He wore one sock and carried a cheap sleeping bag and an aluminum stepladder.

I heard the first winter he slept in people's cars. They'd come out in the morning to start their engines and go back inside while the defrost was roaring and he'd be there asleep across the backseat.

When it got real cold a church tried to help him. They gave him a room in an old downtown hotel that used to be a whorehouse. They got him a job packing boxes and paid him every day and he lasted four days. Then he yelled at one of the old ladies.

"Money don't mean fuckin' nothin'," and threw the dollar bills at her.

The second winter I didn't see him around and thought maybe he'd died, although I didn't think anything could kill him if he could sleep outside all winter on frozen car seats. But then in the spring he showed up again sitting on his stepladder on the corner and I got the story from Jesús. Jesús was a friend of mine. He was the one who figured it out.

Apparently the church folks let him sleep in the church before they got him a room in that downtown hotel.

"What he musta done is searched around," said Jesús, "searched around real good and found them spare keys in the back room and got them copied. Then he musta kept them the whole summer."

Jesús was the janitor at the church. The church had a bell tower and a room up in the belfry. Heated and carpeted.

"Far as I know he musta come back in that cold spell at Thanksgiving. Anyway he started living up there so quiet like and I'm working in there every day and never knew he was there he's so much like a cat. You wouldn't think it seeing him out there on his ladder but he must be because I figure he lived up there more than three months.

"Then one day there was this puddle in the sanctuary. But it's a Monday see, and I know I mopped the night before because the choir sings on Sunday nights.

"That puddle kinda scared me till I just forgot about it thinking maybe it was just Jesus himself because you know they're always saying He's working in mysterious ways, right?

"Anyway he got sloppy and left more puddles and one day I

followed them all the way up the stairs above the sanctuary into that room and pushed open the door and found him. And you know what he was doing? Sleeping. And it's the middle of the day too. Sleeping there on the floor with a Bible for a pillow."

So this hobo moved around through that second spring and one day in May the newspaper ran a picture of him sitting on his stepladder:

Local resident soaking up welcome sunshine. Warm weather expected to last.

They ran that same photo two weeks later but smaller and on the back page. The story said they found seven thousand dollars in cash on his body. They said they didn't know how he got so far out into the prairie. He was sixty-seven miles out there. It was far in the night and the stars were so quiet. The engineer said he blew his horn and started flashing his lights. He said he threw on the brakes making that horrible screech but it was impossible to stop a train quick loaded with coal. The engineer said he couldn't figure it out. This guy had his stepladder set up on the ties in the middle of the rails and he was standing on the very top of it with his sleeping bag balanced on his head like a clown and his arms up in the air.

17

WHEN I got back we were still walking down the tracks. Our arms and faces and necks were burned. We were welted from the bugs. We'd been walking for six days.

By now we were all walking at our own pace, often separated from each other by miles. The land seemed slightly drier, but still no road.

It was early in the morning when I spotted a path. I saw it the way a rib-thin coyote sees a rabbit shooting through the bush. I stripped off my sapling rudder, scrambled down the embankment, swung on and pushed off before the bugs could get me.

It was only a game trail along the railroad but I was ebullient just to be riding again. I rode fast as I could. Faster. Blurried and viscous and pounding my pedals. The ground came up and swept under and fell and away and away and away. I was unweighted and cheating gravity and I knew you could only do it for maybe one second in your whole life because I knew nobody could ever cheat gravity. Even for a second.

I rode for miles when the land unexpectedly sighed and started to roll. Low hills and valleys cornering water and bugs and boredom and floating them away. In a swale where a swamp should have been there was a hayfield. My path ran into the path that reached this desolate hayfield and I knew we would find someone out here and started thinking about food. I let

myself think on what sort of stranger might help us until I
remembered the last village had nothing. Two drunk churls, a
man and a woman who looked the same in soiled clothes and
walked away when we shouted please and then "*khlyep? malako?*"

I pedaled through the hayfield into a grassy, sloping
meadow. Up in the meadow was a crooked log cabin. Narrow
burnt logs with the chinking sliding out and grass grown up to
the windows. There was a fallen picket fence and goats grazing
between the slats. At the far end of the meadow was a creek. I
rode to the bank, laid my bike down, walked into the blue water
and began washing the mud off my face.

Tom came down the path first, his face bobbing like one of
those happy plastic dogs with detached heads and springs for
necks.

"We're riding Marco, *riding!*"

He leapt off his bike and ran wildly into the creek. Torie was
right behind him. She rode directly into the water.

Soon the brothers came out of the birch, their long beards
dribbling. They said nothing. They both immediately recog-
nized the right spot for the fire and began collecting wood.

Natasha pedaled in a few minutes later. She settled her bike
over, pulled her foam pad off the rear rack, spread it out in the
grass, lay down and fell asleep.

When Tanya finally arrived creek water was bubbling in a
black pot hung from a sapling pole and the goats had given up
because we had nothing for them. Tanya was always the slow-
est, always limping into camp last. She dropped her bike, stumbled into the water, lost her balance and sat down on a boulder.
Water swirled around her. She carefully washed off the mud
and dried blood on her legs. Her legs were colorful with
scratches and bruises. She rested on the stone in the creek
hugging her knees for a while, then she was ready.

I walked with her through the goats over the picket fence up
to the cabin. Behind the cabin was a shed. Behind the shed a
garden.

Tanya knocked.

The door opened and a short lady, bald beneath a faded
kerchief, pushed past us.

"*Nyet, nyet, NYET.*" She was screaming.

Tanya skipped around in front of her. "Babushka. *Malako?*"

"*NYET. NYET. Nyet, nyet . . .*" The woman was mumbling and screaming and then mumbling. She hadn't looked at us.

She had a wide forehead, whiskers and few teeth, short meaty arms. I believed she was just another stump of a woman gone mad in Siberia. But then, when Tanya looked away, the old woman's eyes scooted out across her front yard and she saw our bicycles in the grass and knew we couldn't be dangerous.

"Babushka. *Khlyep?*" Tanya held out our crumpled rubles.

The woman spun around, snatched a gray pail off a nail and headed toward the shed.

"Tanya, there's another cabin on the other side of the tracks." She looked at me and smiled.

We walked back to the creek and splashed across mossy stones beneath the railroad tracks. It wasn't a bridge, just a slot in the embankment to let the stream through. On the other side, set back from the water, was a cabin, several sheds and a gray outhouse leaning like a broken thumb. The cabin had a tar-paper roof, shutters nailed shut and a porch vined in with flowers growing tall as trees. There was a colossal sow lounging in a syrupy black puddle, tits dripping, and chickens snapping their heads against the ground.

Down at the end of the porch, in the shade of the flowers, was a man. He was kicked back in a stickwood chair. We walked closer. He was snoring, his head over a log in the cabin wall. He had a big stationary Adam's apple. White bristles stuck out his nose and ears and ran irrationally all down his neck and across his cheeks. He was sleeping with a smile on his face.

"*Privyet,*" Tanya whispered.

He blinked, but didn't raise his head. He just let his sloppy blue eyes roam over Tanya and then me and then back to roaming over Tanya. That was why Tanya was the one who always had to go for food.

"We are bicycling across Siberia." Tanya spoke slowly in her clearest Russian. She held out the rubles.

He didn't move. His long brown brokenveined hands stayed balled around the ends of the armrests. His eyes darted like two identical blue fish. Not at the money, at me.

"Do you have bread? Do you have milk?"

His eyes began to jump and swim.

Suddenly he realized we were hungry. He rocked forward and set down gigantic black hip waders folded over at the knees. His legs lifted him way up. He was like a monument by Giacometti. That giant and that thin. He wore a blue threadbare military suit jacket too small for him. It pulled in his shoulders. Below the breast pocket were five rows of bright square colors.

"*Mozhit byt'!*"

He lowered a hand onto my shoulder and began pushing me toward one of the sheds. When we got there he put his hand on the mossy roof, leaned over and looked inside. I peered in under his arm. It wasn't a shed. It was someone's home. A ratty bed and a pile of brown tomatoes on the floor. In a corner on a table were two loaves of bread. He reached in, grabbed one and hit it against the side of the shed. It made a clunking sound like a block of wood.

"*Daaaa.*" He looked down at me shining his silver teeth. I could smell the alcohol. He grabbed the other loaf and handed them both to Tanya.

"*Spasiba,*" Tanya said. She asked him how much but he waved her away. He was already pushing me back toward his cabin.

"*Spasiba,*" Tanya said again, and then left.

The man and I walked to the porch. He stopped at the stairs, reached down for my hand, and shook it with both of his. His palms were cool and dry and wide as paddles.

"Andrei Nicolai Sudba. *Saldat bal'shoy vayny.*" He said he was a soldier of the Great War. World War I. His eyes seemed to be constantly watering.

"Mark," I said.

He looked concerned. I gave him my full name including my middle name. He was unsatisfied. I didn't know what to say. In desperation I gave my full name adding "*Amirikanski zhurnalist.*" He cheered immediately and rustled the hair on my head. He stepped up through the flowers onto the broken porch, opened the cabin door and motioned me in.

It was dark inside and we were both blinded. We stood beside each other, his hand on my shoulder, until our eyes adjusted.

There was a broken whitewashed hearth on one wall and nothing else. The wooden floor was clean and empty. There was a room adjacent. He moved me through a skewed doorway ducking his head. He wanted me to meet his wife.

She was sitting on a stool. She was an old woman in an apron. She looked very young and made the soldier smile unconsciously. She was peeling potatoes over a bucket. She stood up proudly and reached out her hand. It was rough and warm.

The room smelled like dust and cooked cabbage and old people. It was the middle of the day but the shutters were nailed tight. Light leaked from a bulb hung from the ceiling. Plaster was flaking off in sheets. A picture of Jesus Christ hung on one wall.

There was the giant soldier in his black folded-down hip waders and his tiny flags stapled to his ribs and his wife light and bright as a fawn, and me. There was a half-darned dog wool sock and some battered pots and the knife worn dull and stubby as if the potatoes were stones. There was a metal bed with a wool blanket over rusted springs. On top of the blanket was an army trench coat, lumpy as a body with both arms torn off. I knew they slept here together and always had since after the war and they were as far away as it is possible to get on earth and managed best they knew how.

She held my hand and smiled as if I had a look as though everything wouldn't be all right.

He introduced me forgetting my name but remembering with enthusiasm "*Amirikanski zhurnalist!*"

Her name was Johanna. He said she was from Finland. With his hands, he explained that he married her on the last day of the Great War when it was snowing and everyone was so happy, and smiled the way an old man smiles at someone who has loved him anyway.

He began to tell her that I was hungry. I looked at the potatoes and the blunt knife and broken walls and felt sick with myself.

His eyes were watering like ponds and hers were almonds on me. I tried to let my hand slip from hers and then she noticed and let go easily smiling as if she had let go a skipping stone.

"*Nyet, nyet, khlyep, dastatachna,*" I protested. Over and over I said the bread was enough and "*spasiba, spasiba*" and good-bye and "*spasiba*" and finally slipped out and ran down the porch into the creek.

*   *   *

The madwoman had brought milk and cucumbers. She had dug the cucumbers from her garden. The milk was warm in a gray pail. She was standing on the fallen picket fence, a goat nudging the palm of her hand.

Torie handed me a stiff piece of bread with chunks of cucumber. I ate it, finished the milk, walked over and put the pail back in the babushka's hand.

Pavel was flat in the grass beside Natasha. Both were asleep. Pavel and Natasha now slept twelve hours every night and slept at every break.

Fyodor was resting on his side in the grass reading the Bible. He had combed his hair in the creek. It was dripping into his beard and then into his Bible which he read all the time but never said a word about one way or the other.

Tom had Tanya's bike upside down in the grass. He was trying to teach her something about her bike. He had been doing this since the beginning. He had that kind of patience. Tanya was acting as if she were paying attention.

Then the old man came sloshing up the creek out from under the railroad tracks. He had both arms held high as if the stream were deep. In each hand was a gunnysack.

He walked up into the grass past the fire, stopped in front of me and put down the sacks. From one he lifted out a big white plastic bag. He forced it into my hands. From the other he set out a can of horse meat, a jar of homemade jam and a dozen peeled potatoes.

Then he stood back up giantlike and his medals and his drippy eyes hung over our heads like something we couldn't change. Like history.

He began his speech. I thought it would be a long speech because I could smell the alcohol. Tanya sat in the grass and translated.

"In the Great War we had no sugar. I got a letter once from my mother who said my sister had tried to bring me sugar. But I never saw her. The letter said she left to try to bring me sugar and never came back. She was my sister and she took care of me before I went to war. I was fourteen and she was thirteen."

And he stopped.

He wouldn't take any of what he had brought. Not even a

cup of tea with a spoonful of sugar. He stepped off in the grass and watched.

The brothers and Natasha wolfed the can of horse meat and Torie whipped up jam sandwiches. We saved the potatoes for dinner.

Tanya began talking to him and translating for us and he came closer but stayed standing up, his military jacket pinching his shoulders and his rusty medals holding him up there as if they stuck right through his ribs into the sky.

He said he came here after the war because back then the men and women who worked on the railroad were paid well. They were paid with food. They got winter boots. He told us about a time when a train derailed and he stole as many boxes of crackers as he could carry. This made him laugh and come over and grab me with his veiny hands and growl and act as if he wanted to wrestle. He told us about how deep the snow was every winter and how cold it got and how much wood he had to chop and how he'd split open his foot with an ax once and his wife had been away working shoveling snow off the rails so his son had had to stitch it up with sewing thread and then his voice trailed off.

Suddenly he seemed tired. He sat down beside us. He said he had another story. He paused. This is a story about my son, he said. He said his son had looked just like him, and pointed to Tom. He tried to smile and tried to start the story but his eyes began spilling into the ground and his face bit itself so he just sat there very quiet.

It was late and we had to go. We started packing up. He sat and watched. Then he rose and strode down into the stream and vanished under the railroad tracks.

Our bikes were packed and we were about to leave when he came back. He marched up out of the stream and went straight to Tom and ruffled his huge hands through Tom's hair. Then he drew something from his suit jacket pocket. It was a small red-and-white plastic rocket with one broken fin. He pressed the rocket into Tom's hand.

Tom held it carefully. He stared at it, turning it in his hand. Then he looked at me and whispered, "Bike God." He knew I understood.

A bike God is a talisman. It is something you can only get

when you are riding. It must be a gift of the journey. You can't buy it. You can't know what it is before you get it. It just comes.

Tom was red and the old man was watering and rocking back on his heels with his chest swelled way up.

"*Spasiba*," Tom said solemnly and reached out his hand. The old man leaned down and smothered Tom's hand in both of his. Then he motioned for Tom to hold the rocket up to his eye. Tom did.

"It's a kaleidoscope," Tom shouted. "And guess what! Yury Gagarin's in there."

Yury Gagarin is a famous man, a famous traveler. He went as far away as you can get. He was the Soviet Union's first cosmonaut.

18

Our path ended the next day and we had to walk the rails again. We walked for three days.

Then, once upon an evening, a gravel road rose out of the swamp and carried us away from the railroad. We were overwhelmed. The road climbed a mountain and descended in long slow curves into a small valley.

There was a wide river. The soft banks touched both sides of the valley. Over a buckled log bridge higgledypiggledy in the hillside grass was a village. Tilting and lilting little log cabins. Baby blue or forest green or orange with matching picket fences.

There was an island in the river. It split the snowy water like a wedge. You could reach it off the bridge. We put our tents beneath giant pines on the island.

Pavel and Fyodor cut two Y-shaped saplings and drove them into the ground with the flat of the ax. They cut a pot pole and laid it across the top. Underneath they built a fire. Their eyes watered from the smoke and their beards caught sparks.

Torie collected the food each of us was carrying. She sliced the block of bread and the tomato and peeled three eggs.

Natasha sat down in the grass on the riverbank. She washed her face and hands and watched her reflection. She did not smile even to herself.

Tom began an operation on Fyodor's bike. It was heart sur-
gery performed in the field. He laid the bike down, made it
comfortable, and arranged the few small tools we had on an oily
rag. He was inside quickly, his hands knowledgeable and delicate and bloodied. He was humming.

Tanya and I gathered a large pile of firewood, then crossed
the bridge into the village. Up a lumpy mud street past a flapping flock of geese, Tanya yelled to a crooked man shingling a
crooked roof.

"Sir, do you have milk?"

He pointed over all the other crooked wood roofs and we
went in that direction. We found a warty woman with a flat nose
who wouldn't answer her window. We heard people shuffling
behind shut cabin shutters and dogs shunting behind fences.
Then a man on a muckled motorcycle, a rakish cap down over
his eyes and a wibbly sidecar by his side, slowed by.

"*Malako?*" Tanya shouted.

He pluttered to a stop and stepped uncertainly off.

"*Da,*" he croaked.

He was drunk and yawing. He sold us a jar of goat milk.

Word had spread by the time we returned to the island.
Children were everywhere. Dirty curious fearless children.
They ran wild. Barefoot or booted in shorts and newspaper
hats, shouting to get our attention then hiding behind the giant
trees like elves.

But not all of them were children. Some were manboys.
Those queer violent satyrs boys become just before they are
men. The manboys kept their distance. They were big as we
were and tougher. You could see it in their eyes and in the way
they smoked and spit and folded their bigfisted arms.

"*Ukhaditye!*" Fyodor shouted. Go away! He said they could
hurt us. When we squatted by the campfire for dinner he was
angry. The elves and satyrs were spying on us from the forest.
He jerked to his feet and swung his ax in the sky and howled
like a lunatic. The little ones ran off—stopping suddenly, staring back, then running on through the trees. The manboys
walked away slow, their muscled backs straight, an eye cocked
over their shoulders.

After dinner Fyodor and I left the island and walked back
into the village. Tanya and I had discovered something extraor-

dinary, an opera house. It had four white pillars, broad open steps and rose far above the cabins. When we got there the sky had turned a plum color and the columns were pink.

We went up the steps. Movie posters garish and gripping were stapled to the wooden doors. We went inside. The lobby was cold as a cave. The tile on the floor was broken and the bars on the ticket booth were bent. Once it was an opera house, now it was a theater. A movie was about to begin.

A woman wide as she was tall, hidden inside an armor of sweaters, padded toward us. Fyodor paid and she took us by the elbows through the curtain into darkness. She pushed us into seats.

The movie splashed light across the purple walls and up onto the vaulted ceiling and through the chandeliers into the balcony. It rent the room, rolling over the rows of wooden seats. Far away, on the other side of the empty auditorium, were two figures.

It was an unclear movie. Arabic dubbed in Russian. It was set in a hillside village in a small valley. The blind moon sailed in and out. It was a famous children's fable. There was a cave in the mountains and treasure inside the cave. There was good and bad and greed and lust. Scimitars lunged and blood splattered the theater but I was numb with fatigue and had to lay my head back.

I drifted, then fell headfirst into the fable. I went clashing and hiding and hunting. I was the way you are when you try to understand you are asleep and it is not real but it is.

And then it ended. We waited in the dark. Dark so deep dark you are dreaming or completely awake and there is no difference.

A shadow approached. The woman held the candle and the flaming wax dripped on her knuckles and she pushed us out a door by the stage.

Moonless. The earth sheathed inside the night like a wooden sword. We were silent and sightless and drugged by the nightness. We stumbled back to the bridge and fell down onto our island. We could hear the river murmuring.

Fyodor went to his tent. I found my bike and tied it to my tent and struggled into my bag.

Everything was black. I lay back flat. When I was warm, my

body decoupled. My eyes sank into my head like stones to the bottom of a black pool and I was asleep and running and riding and fending and fighting. Ali Baba I was and I flayed the evil forty. I found the treasure. I vanquished. I felt the glistening whistling of triumph and lust but, but . . . something was wrong. I couldn't see it. I was blinded. A scimitar through my head and my eyes full of blood but I could feel it. Something *wrong*. Whispering. Steps. A knife. A knife but I couldn't see it. I could hear it flashing and feel it slicing but I was blind and could not move and heard the clicking and running and then I was naked standing in cold grass.

"Thieves!"

My bike was gone. There was an innocent blind moon. Violet purple light was falling into the forest.

Fyodor appeared. He had his ax. I put on my shorts and shoes and we became silent. Vengeful. Searching.

We loped in large circles around my tent. Running through the dark on the island running. We found the tracks. The tracks went to the bridge, then over the river and through the woods.

I was liquid and hot and sweating and we were running and running graceful and catlike. The tracks were barely visible in the moonlight but we were heated by instinct and hunting, our snouts close to the ground eyes on the track running through the dark trees for a long time and we were not tired. We knew it was to the end. We could hunt all morning and all day and all night forever.

We stopped. Hid behind the trees.

Preparing and crouching and breathing and breathing thinking they have a knife they were cunning they knew what they were doing they had been watching following silent and hard and merciless.

They invalided me. I begin to tremble. I feel the claw.

There is my bicycle, stripped and lying in the purple forest. There are two rough manboys with blazing eyes. They see us. They turn, and wait.

Fyodor steps into the moonlight with his ax. He does not move. He does not look at me. It is my bicycle.

I attack. I feel it inside my skin. The knife comes through the air but the manboy drops and blood flies and the other fights but feels the heat and hate and loses screaming falling broken in the face and I lift him and strike again and purple vomit covers the forest floor.

Once upon a morning the sun rises. Darkness gone like it never was. The police are there in the valley. They wear black boots. They have evil police eyes. They punch and kick the thieves.

Two women are there in the mud in rags wailing and screeching for their bloodied broken sons.

In the light, I see they are only Russian boys with mothers.

19

WE LEFT the island and rolled quietly over a mountain and down into the next valley. For two days we pedaled valley to valley. Often the road paralleled the railroad. It was not a good road, but we were riding and that was enough.

Once, following a puddled track through dense timber, we broke into a remarkable meadow. Flowers neck high. A forest of flowers, their yellow heads nodding atop tall blue stems. The smell enveloped us.

Tanya had been left behind but the Soviets refused to wait. Tom, Torie and I stopped where the path looped near the railroad embankment. We dismounted, wobbled around on tired legs, and fell into the flowers. We were asleep quickly.

A heavy sound woke us sometime later. It rumbled the ground and we sprang to our feet. It was the unmistakable sound. Train sound. Heaving huge lowbellied train shumbling around the bend into the meadow.

The train came toward us slow, groaning and slowing, and stopped, right beside us, big as a ship. It wasn't a freight train. All the cars had windows with shades like square eyes with sleepy eyelids. Every car had a red star in the middle of its flank. It was a Trans-Siberian train, the famous Moscow-to-Vladivostok tourist train.

It was bigger than a village. We knew inside there was more

food than in a village and clean sheets and clean water and toilet paper and foggy foreigners and that the train would do in a week what we were taking three seasons to attempt.

We stared at the dining car. We were hungry. We were thinking the same thing: maybe we could buy food.

"What do you think?" Tom said.

"I don't think we need it," I said.

"I agree," said Torie.

So we just watched.

The train was close and silent. Above the bigheaded flowers, through the blueing reflections and the shades, we could see people eating. They were using silverware and drinking from china teacups. They began pointing to us through the glass as if they were on one of those miniature trains that trolls through a zoo, or perhaps in the dark hall of one of those marine museums and had just come around a corner and spotted us, aquanauts, swimming in one of the tanks.

We waved. They waved back and smiled. We heard creaking and prying and a door at the end of the dining car levered open. Two heads popped out into the perfumed air. A man and a woman. They looked unreal to us, like dolls, so well-washed and welldressed we could almost smell the soap. Hair combed teeth cleaned lipstick jewelry.

"*Zdrastvutye, kak vy pazhyvayitye?*" the man said.

Tom said hello back in Russian and told him we were fine.

"*Shto, vy delayitye?*"

Tom laughed. "He asked us what we are doing. What should I say?"

"Tell him we are train robbers," Torie said under her breath. "What else? Tell him we're bicycling across Siberia."

The tourists both gasped and the man shouted, "You speak English?!"

We said yes and moved closer to the train. Tom and the man began a conversation about bicycling. The man was from the Netherlands.

I thought: Of all the people we will never meet on all the passenger trains crossing the thousands of meadows of Siberia, we meet a Dutchman: a man from the land of flowers and bicycles.

"But how did you get permission?" the man asked. Tom told him.

"But there isn't a road all the way across?"

"Yes, we know."

"Well then, how do you manage in the swamp?"

Tom explained.

"Village to village, then?" the man said. Tom nodded.

The Dutchman's face lit up. He was pleased and astonished.

The woman spoke. "But where are you from?"

She was a beautiful young woman, a brunette in a smooth dress. Her teeth were bright white. She wasn't from Holland, her accent didn't sound like that. I realized she was from the United States.

We each gave our hometown.

"You must be mad! Bicycling across Siberia!"

We looked at each other. We had forgotten what Americans were like. Before any of us could speak she said, "What a ridiculous struggle! What could you possibly see that we aren't seeing?"

Tom's face dropped. He couldn't respond. "Mark, why don't you answer that?"

I couldn't. Torie whispered in my ear. "We *should* have said we were train robbers. She watches TV. She's on a train. She would understand that."

I looked up. The woman was waiting for an answer. She pushed her hair back with her hand. She was wearing several rings.

The engines down the meadow started up, coughing, blowing. The train started to creak and move. Slow at first, inching away, faster and faster.

The woman began waving and shouting good luck and things like that but I caught the eyes of the Dutchman. He was pulling the door closed. When he saw me, he suddenly leaned desperately far out and shouted.

"You're *not* mad," he threw his hand in the air, "you're brilliant."

20

W E WHEELED into another village late that afternoon. Actually it was a town. The log homes had been bulldozed into a heap and tenements erected. The walls of the tenements had red placards of Him incarnate as the leather-gloved welder. There was a long outhouse in front of each tenement.

I had to go. There were two doors. I went in one while a fat woman with her daughter went in the other. There were six holes on the men's side and shit on the walls. I could hear the fat woman breathing heavily. I heard her hike up her dress and the scratchy sound that makes and then the splashing but I knew she wasn't sitting because there was shit everywhere. I wasn't sitting either. I was holding myself up.

A man came in. He wore a wide tie and shook my hand. He spread a newspaper over the hole next to me and punched a hole in it businesslike and sat down.

"*Etot gorat stroil Stalin,*" he said. Stalin made this town.

I didn't know what to say.

"*Byl viliki chilavyek.*" Stalin was a great man.

I looked at him on the hole beside me. He was an older man. He was staring straight ahead.

I finished and offered him some of my toilet paper. He took a handful and said thank you. I went out, then turned and knocked on the door. I asked him where the town grocery store was.

"*Kaneshna*," he shouted, "*Vy dalzhni eetee sivodnya v magazin. Magazin yest' sakhar.*" Of course. You must go to the store. The store has sugar today.

That made me laugh.

"*Magazin yest' sakhar!*" he shouted again and kicked the door.

We quickly bicycled to the store. No villages had had sugar, sugar was precious. Sugar was like gold. People robbed for sugar.

The store did have sugar. We stood in a long line. A woman in the line again told us this town was made by Stalin. She was proud. A woman behind her said someone in this town knew someone who knew someone who actually did know someone so today they had sugar.

"We are blessed," someone said.

We bought seven three-pound boxes, one for each of us, and bread. We wrapped the boxes in clear plastic bags and left town.

We rode fifty-three miles that day and fifty-nine miles the next day. The forest all around us was a foot deep in water but we didn't care. We had begun to believe we were on a road. We thought we could forget about the railroad. We were on a road and we had grown up believing roads went somewhere.

It rained that night. We slept beside the railroad tracks and the rain dampened the sound of the trains.

It was still raining in the morning. Cold gray winterish rain. We couldn't get a fire started. We loaded our wet belongings.

We saddled up and rode about three hundred yards, around a small bend, and the road stopped. Just stopped, as if it had been lopped off like an arm or a leg.

You would think sleeping that close to tragedy we would feel it in our dreams but we didn't. That's how strong hope is. We were becoming Russian but I didn't know it yet.

We walked our bikes into the water. The water was thigh deep and freezing and dimpling from the hard rain. We went straight for the tracks, slopped up the embankment and started walking.

Pavel's rear tire blew up almost immediately. It sounded like a gunshot.

"*Mudnya! Amirikanski vilosiped,*" he roared. Shit American bike. He threw it down on the rails.

I checked the tire. It had not popped from the glass or wire that was everywhere along the railroad. The sidewall had blown not the tread. Pavel's brake pads were bent upward. For the past three days whenever he had braked, the pads had clamped against the sidewall of the tire rather than the rim.

"Pavel, you are a fucking idiot," Tom said. But he spoke in English. Tom had told Pavel repeatedly to adjust his brakes. He had told him this would happen if he didn't.

Our spare tires were in Chita which was somewhere we no longer understood. Tom gave Pavel a needle and dental floss. Pavel sat down on the tracks and angrily stitched up the rip in the sidewall. He stitched it up poorly. We took turns standing over him like an umbrella.

Then we again began pushing our bicycles between the gleaming rails in the black rain. We walked no more than three hundred yards before the stitches popped and the tire exploded again. I heard the report. I felt like punching Pavel in the stomach. I whipped around and there, there was a strange man on the tracks. He was standing in the rain in red suspenders and baggy wet clothes. He shook my hand.

"*Mokry dyen', da?*"

Tanya came up the tracks and began talking to him.

"He wants me to tell you he said, 'Wet day, huh.'" She laughed.

The man had a curly brown beard and wore a sopping fedora. He'd heard the tire explode and thought it was a gunshot and walked down to the tracks from his cabin to check it out. He invited us to his cabin.

It was raining winter rain in summer so hard it seemed even the forest would float away. We'd made about a quarter of a mile in three hours which meant it would take us around nine thousand days or twenty-five years to reach Leningrad, which was somewhere we no longer understood anyway. We accepted.

The cabin was in the woods on a little hill. It had a shed attached to the back wall. One side of the shed was open. Inside were six men crowded at a table covered with a red-and-white checked tablecloth. The men were big. They were eating. When we came through the trees they stood up, knocking over the benches, and stepped out into the rain. They shook our hands and pushed us into the shed.

"*Dobra pozhalavat.*" Welcome.

The man who had led us here squeezed the water from his beard and moved us close to the wood stove, a radiating black box covering a third of the grass floor. A pipe stuck up through the roof of the shed.

The men in the rain shifted foot to foot like horses. They joked with each other.

We hunkered so close to the stove we baked our soaked clothes. We stripped and hung the clothes on nails. By then the man in suspenders with a fedora and a gun had had one of the men standing outside wash the plates in the rain. He reset the table himself, placing a hard-boiled egg and a can of sardines on each plate.

"Now you must sit and eat," he said.

So we did. The men watched.

Afterward, Pavel took a four-inch section of spare tire I kept in my repair kit and nested it inside his bad tire where the sidewall had blown. He sewed it in slowly using tight stitches and yards of dental floss while Tanya asked the man in the fedora questions.

"She wants to know who we are," said the man. The men grinned.

"Well, we are gold miners. We live in these mountains and we search for gold and we take care of strange cyclists whenever they drop in."

A smile moved through us.

"We serve them poisoned sardines and eggs from sick chickens and force them to sit by our wood stove when it is raining."

One of the men slapped his side and shook his head throwing off water like a dog.

"We live in this cabin and cook out here in this shed. We play cards, even when the snow is so deep we have to make walls out of it. And sometimes . . . we rob trains."

He had made us tea on the wood stove. He was pouring us each a cup. He nodded to one of the men and the man went into the cabin and came back out with a small blue tin that made a popping sound in the rain.

The man in the fedora pulled off the lid and solemnly set the tin in the middle of the table. He looked at us. I thought he was going to say something, but he didn't.

The tin had sugar in it. There were only a few chunks left. We used them all for our tea, then it was time to go. Pavel's tire was repaired and we were warm and dry again.

We stepped out into the rain and the men shook our hands. We picked up our bicycles and waited until the Soviets had gone back down to the tracks.

Tom nodded to Torie and I held her bike. She stepped inside the shed and put a clear plastic bag on top of the tin box and we left.

Tom Freisem

Torie Scott receiving flowers in
a small Siberian village

Author in a Siberian village

Tanya Kirova

Natasha Traviynskay

Pavel (left) *and*
Fyodor Konyukhov

Tom Freisem in Leningrad at
the end of the journey

Pushing through the balota

Bicycle and Siberian home

Typical campsite

Tom Freisem, Tanya Kirova, Torie Scott, and author (left to right) *at the Baltic Sea*

Babushka

Babushkas

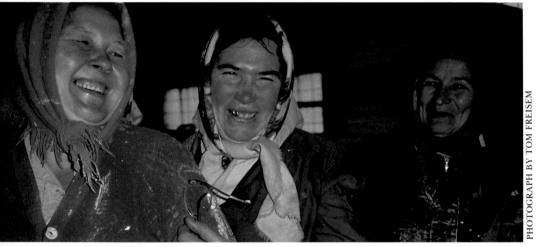

Leah

Russian girls

Russian children

Russian cowboy

Russian man

21

Back to the tracks. Back walking in the rain fondling our dark thoughts in our damp heads pushing and pushing jumping off the tracks like rats when a train comes then pushing and pushing until we're inanimate and stumbly and time has slowed.
   Like a heartbeat right before death   thunkthnk

    thunkthnk   thunkthnk

so slowed you can't keep straight if a minute has passed or an hour or an hour is a minute or maybe a day or a day a week or a week a year and you pray for your head to behead itself quickly before you start counting railroad ties because counting ties is the road to madness because you know you go two a second when they're spaced far apart and three a second when they're close together and there are 86,400 seconds in a day and whatever you do you must never start counting when suddenly you have vanished off the face of the earth and won't look down can't look down and look down just for a second and hear "ninety-two, ninety-three, ninety-four" and bite your lip till it bleeds because you know pain is so simple and so incontrovertible it will keep you sane. You have learned that from the Russians.
   Days later a train stops. Not a whole train just an engine.

Workers in smutty orange suits standing on the steps smoking and holding on to the rail.

"Want a lift?"

We're far below on legs black with bruises.

"Hey, you got ears? Want a lift?"

We will drag back up onto the tracks when they chug off and keep walking and in a few hours they'll be a hundred miles on where maybe there are roads and towns like the world should be and we'll still be a week away just a few miles farther down the tracks than we can see right now, camped in birch trees, while they're eating in log cabins telling a story that no one believes about how they saw folks with bicycles in the *balota.*

This goes through all of us before someone, Fyodor or Tom or Tanya or I, blinks and answers.

"*Nyet, spasiba.*"

Because by now we have learned something else from the Russians and it's down deep inside us and it is our secret: Distance is nothing. It can evaporate like water and time. Now we know there is no distance on earth too far. We could walk any distance. We could walk forever.

One day we meet a man standing in hay. His huskies howl with their noses in the air. There is a dogsled in the loft of a barn. The man has a narrow head and a short body. He is whorled around a handmade rake.

The man lives alone with his dogs. They romp about on the roof of his cabin barking. We take water from his well and Fyodor unfolds our map. The man gets excited and points here and there on the paper. Half his fingers are stumps. He is looking for where we must be. He is seeing his world for the first time from the sky. It makes him laugh. The map is upside down.

"*Nyet.*" He can't find where we are. He has news for us though.

"There's a road," he says.

"How far?" Fyodor asks.

"Not so far. Just around the mountain. Only go there in winter with my dogs. Starts at the village."

"Have you been on the road?"

"Nope." The rake is holding the man up. "Goes down to a big river though, know that."

"You're sure?"

"Sure."

We get back up on the tracks. We have our own faith and don't believe him. We have faith in deception. We have faith in the cmasculatability of all things on earth.

But around the mountain there is a village. The tracks run right through it. And there is the road, going south out of the village.

"No one knows where the road goes."

Tanya is speaking to a babushka bent over picking cucumbers.

"Someone must know where the road goes."

"Why?" The babushka is puzzled.

We find another babushka in the village. She is milking a goat.

"It goes to a great river."

"What river?"

The babushka throws her hands in the air. We buy the goat milk.

We find a man painting the door to his cabin and show him our map. He looks at it carefully, his fingers dripping with blue paint.

"We are not on this map."

"Where are we?"

The man laughs. He points to somewhere beyond the map in the void where anything could happen.

"We are off the map."

"Then where does the road go?" Tanya asks.

He laughs again. "Further."

There is no discussion. Just to be bicycling again, we would take the road even if it dropped into hell.

We holler and clap and spur out of town. We ride hard all day through little mountains. At nightfall we camp just off the road beside a creek and build a big campfire and talk late into the night under singing stars and decide we are the luckiest travelers on earth because riding for just one afternoon has let hope grow back up inside us because we are human and hope is like that, like a seed in your stomach no matter what silly faith you say you have.

We ride all the next day. Through hilly pine and birch country. No one is on this road but us. We don't care. It's just a dirt thing no wider than a stream but it goes furling and curling up down around and back up again and we're riding and that's all we ever wanted. We start thinking again, thinking this may be a real road like those fairy-tale roads that actually go somewhere in life.

In evening the road is climbing into mountains. There have been no villages. We have seen no people. There have been no turnoffs, only this road rising through the scented forest into the mountains all by itself.

Light becomes lavender. We keep climbing and the road begins to switchback. Eventually we stitch up through the trees to a pass where the road runs along the edge of a ridge. For a mile we can see over both sides. It's like looking down at the world from a lavender cloud. We can gaze over the side we came from and down the unknown side where we're going. Both sides look the same. Uninhabited and green and deep and hazy. But the sides don't feel the same because we have our hope up high now. We think we are escaping. We think we have suffered.

Then the road falls off the ridge on the unknown side and just keeps falling, as if there's no bottom. Dropping and dropping. We twirl in evil corkscrew curves with edges that peel off into dark space. We're speeding and skidding and our brakes are squealing and the road just keeps falling.

Then the road begins to dwindle. Narrower and less shoulder after each curve. It is unspeakable.

I can't see everyone but I can hear them.

"*No.*"

The road is sinister, twirling and dropping, thinning.

"*No. No!*"

Now we're falling. Curves and curves and curves until the road debouches down into a valley and turns to mud. It writhes through a wicked thicket. It turns to a trail. We are sick. Trees begin to cave in and swamp and mud pour around us and we can't see each other and the trail keeps limping and limping and we're floundering and foundering cuts on our faces branches at our throats slivers broken off in our heads "*NO!*"

We break clear.

The river.

22

I LOST MY first bike when I was five. For the next six years I was crippled and I knew it.

But Dad had a bike.

Pythagoras, that's what Dad called him. Big and heavy as a draft horse. Gleaming black with balloon tires and white rims, handlebars wide as longhorns, fenders stiff enough to sit on. Pythagoras had a mind of his own. He was old, older than Steve and I put together.

We weren't allowed to ride Pythagoras. Dad thought he was too big for us. He didn't know we already took turns practicing on the grass in the backyard, riding the great thing in big slow circles. Mom would watch from the kitchen window and rap on the glass when we were in danger of being discovered.

Steve and I shared a bedroom in the basement. It was down there, in the whaleblack nights of boylong summers, lying next to each other beneath the blankets, that we'd talk. We always talked about the titan with one eye. He lived in a fabled junkyard far out in the prairie. They said he had naked rutting blue women on his chest and hair on his back and a shotgun the size of a cannon. But what scared us was his hyena dog. A beast vicious beyond belief. Hackled shoulders, slavering bonecracking snout.

One night, when we'd grown brave from all the talking, we decided we must go.

In the morning we asked Mom what day it was. She had to look on the calendar on the refrigerator because summer was like that for her too.

"Friday."

"Tomorrow!" Steve whispered. We slipped out into the garage.

Tomorrow Dad would be gone. Every Saturday morning early he went fishing. He was a serious fisherman. It was a grave and sacrosanct affair as it is for all serious fishermen. Whenever Steve and I went along we had to squelch the urge, bad as an itch, to send a stone whizzing over the morning pink water. That was too hard on us so we stopped going.

Pythagoras was in the garage. We oiled his chain until it dripped on the cement and pumped up the tires hard as horse legs. From Dad's toolbox we stole a hammer, a screwdriver, and pliers. We shoved them nervously into a gym bag and rushed the bag under our bed. We were throbbing with excitement. We didn't think we could wait all the way to tomorrow.

That night the feeling was still inside us like a bellyache we could forget as long as we were moving but felt all over the minute we lay still under the covers. It was a yearning. It made us tingle. Made us so hot we had to throw the blankets back. Steve and I were ordinary boys, we willed for one thing in life: to be adventuring. Going where we didn't know where for no other reason than the going.

Of course we had our excuse—like all great explorers we intended to bring back treasure. But even then, when I was nine and Steve was eight and the world was bigger than it ever would be again, we understood. We knew instinctually what the timorous gray writers of our history books didn't: No explorer worth half his legend ever went anywhere for treasure—gold or silver or fame. Not one. We knew only scoundrels set out for such tripe and they never survived anyway, disease or spears or a fateful snake would always fell the shallow-hearted. We understood Odysseus and Columbus and Sir Richard Burton. We knew Marco Polo. We knew they had had to appease their tiny-headed benefactors, but their desire was pure.

Seemed like forever to fall asleep that night. Whispering

then quiet then one of us disturbing the blackness saying something about what would happen or what could happen just as the other one was falling away and getting both of us shuddering again as if tomorrow were bigger than Christmas or the last day of school.

Maybe just two minutes after we stopped talking for good we heard Dad's bony feet creaking and the toilet flushing and not too long later the door slammed. We plucked on our shorts, grabbed the bag of tools and stole out to the garage. Pythagoras was sleeping. He woke when we flicked up the kickstand.

It was a darkling blue-pink dawn in our flat prairie town. Cloudless and radiant like the first day of all famous voyages. Steve climbed into the saddle and I swung over the bar onto the pedals and we were off.

We took the back way. Nothing moved or breathed but us, borne effortlessly to the edge of town. We went first down streets we already knew—the smells and the colors and which dogs were loose—then on into alien country with no curbs and dark houses. We rode through the trailer court where all the kids were tough and sinewy and played in the sagebrush. The trailer court was the border, the edge of the known world.

We rode straight out into the prairie.

It was glowing. It was unexplored and unfathomable and vast. We cantered up and over a hill, and town vanished behind us. We rode across a no-man's-land, spooking a herd of antelope. They bolted away in a cloud of dust. Then, atop the next hill, we saw it: the junkyard, acres of rusted metal skeletons sinking into the prairie. The trail went to the barbwire. We came up very slow, hardly moving slow, and stopped.

Steve jumped off and I let Pythagoras down easy. We fell flat on our bellies, clutched the barbwire, pulled ourselves under and went scrunching forward between the behemoths. I knew Steve was so scared he might wet himself. I looked backward down my legs and his face was at my feet and he smiled but he was white as milk. But we kept going. Dirt in our shorts and hightops, stickers stuck in our froggy knees, our fingernails trembling in the cool ground.

We were on our bellies in a graveyard so sacred and dangerous we could taste it in our mouths like a penny. The corpses were unburied and enormous and torn apart. Eyes big as our heads hanging out. Mouths propped open. Viscera and appendages scattered everywhere.

We couldn't believe we were here and how easy it had been, just riding away from home and keeping riding and riding without thinking and then you were there, on the edge, and then just keeping going and quick as you would want you were out there, clear, clear out there, off the map.

I was moving fast and careless and accidentally kicked a hood set up sideways and it boomed. Our blood stopped. Our breathing stopped. We were frozen as lizards, listening, heads cocked with one eye boring into a blue sky and our ears long as our legs.

We stayed like that for a long while.

Nothing. Nothing!

We moved on. There was great loot everywhere. Mirrors and old tools and huge screws and ancient clothes. We went peeking through the bones of a bailer and scrambling over an orange bus and operating the gears inside a crane with a broken neck. We jerked steering wheels and pumped pedals and saw a field mouse duck down through seat springs. We climbed into the stomach of one brute just to examine the innards. Seemed stupid to us. So big and complex compared to Pythagoras.

Then we remembered our mission. We hopped down and crawled under the axle. Steve removed the tools from the gym bag and slid up next to the hub. Using the pliers, he tugged at the metal housing. It popped out. We both peered inside, knocking heads.

There they were: ball bearings. All stuck in a big mucky ring like black pearls in a necklace.

"Steelies," Steve gasped.

Everyone was winning with them at school, smashing the marbles clean out of the circle. If we got home with just this one great gooey ring we would be heroes and rich.

The ring had to be hammered out. It was going to make noise but we were fearless now. Steve set the screwdriver just right and smacked it. There was a loud twang and the bearing cage burped out black grease. He hit it again and the report cracked over the prairie and suddenly, suddenly we heard the worst sound in all the unknown world: the bark of the hyena dog. It cut us in half as if the windshield had dropped from the truck.

It came again, deep and ghastly. We were quivering. We wanted to cry. Steve took the pliers and yanked the bearing cage and it fell out in his hand and he turned to me and tried to speak but no words came out. We spun around and started to run and stopped. We spun in a circle. Again. Again. I felt like vomiting and shitting and exploding all at once because I knew we were lost and I knew the bluntheaded hyena dog all death muscle and dripping teeth was searching for us.

Steve stood waiting and shaking uncontrollably while I got up onto the cab of the truck. I stayed on my stomach and looked around. Heaps of crashed and rusted red iron and then yellow prairie endless in every direction until the blue stopped it. I was dizzy with terror and sweating everywhere my neck twitching fingers fainting eyes rolling out of my head praying please PLEASE!

Just as I saw the barbwire fence a clattering howling scraping ripped the flesh off the morning and there was the rabid hyena dog shot straight up on the roof of a car pawing the iron and the one-eyed tattooed titan beside him with his cannon and I didn't see anymore shattered inside as in a nightmare Steve and I screaming soundlessly running and running the cannon exploding metal splintering glass ricocheting around us running side by side our boy heads back and elbows pumping and the hyena dog roaring and bounding and there's the barbwire and we're under and Pythagoras is spinning and charging and snorting.

Then, like diving into warm water, we were sliding down through the trailer court laughing. Laughing hysterically the way brothers can make each other laugh. Whooping. Steve waving the greasy ring of ball bearings and neither of us realizing yet that we'd forgotten Dad's tools.

23

WE CAMPED by the river. The smoke from our fire carried out over the black current and we slept without hope or dread. Still.

In the morning magenta fog caped the valley. We were out of food, but food had become like distance and time—we could get along without it. We found a sandy, trackless path beside the river and took it upstream. West.

Blue mountains rose out on both sides of the water as if we were in a fjord. We pedaled silently through inky fog up long narrow fields of grass. The grass was wet and high and the path went steady. Not fast or hurried, just asked us to come along and we came.

We passed into a bizarre forest—a forest of plants, marijuana plants. They were green and bushy and eight feet tall, trunks thick as a man's wrist, large spiky leaves scenting the air.

"Damn . . . Mark."

I couldn't see Tom. He was just ahead of me gliding through the fog.

"I know."

"Where *are* we?"

"I don't know."

Late in the day the river cleaved through a mountain creating a canyon. The walls of the canyon were sheer and intraversable. The path veered north, wandering up through a pine forest. Riding was easy. We rose above the fog and yellow light came streaming through the branches. We might have spoken to each other but nothing needed saying. The path went up to a small pass and fell into a mountain valley.

It was a bluish-green valley. A creek came out of the distant woods, pigtailed through the great meadow, then gurgled back into the forest. The air was light up here. Warm and light. Far away we could see a cabin. It took some time to ride to it.

It was a cabin built with care, everything true and square, joints tight as knuckles. There were honey boxes in the grass on one side of the house and a corral with a big barn on the other.

Farther up the valley we could see a large horse and people working. We bicycled through the high grass until we reached the patch they had cut.

The father stepped determinedly off a large canvas blanket and walked toward us. He was a big man light on his feet. He wore leather boots that came up to his knees, baggy pants and a white shirt.

"*Dobra pozhalavat.*"

He shook the hand of each of us firmly, as if we were relatives come thousands of miles. His face was tanned through to the bone. He had a remarkable black mustache that spilled down to his chest. He asked us to please sit down with him.

The canvas blanket was spread out beside a small fire. The mother, peering at us from inside a black scarf, sat on a stool boiling tea over the flames.

The father pulled from a cloth sack a round loaf of bread. The loaf was almost two feet across. He slipped a knife out from behind his back and began sawing the bread into chunks. The blade of the knife was so large it looked as if it had been made from a broken broadsword. He handed out the pieces of bread then passed around a metal cup of tea.

"Where are you coming from?"

Fyodor spoke for us at first, but his answers were one-word answers. The man turned his eyes on Fyodor. We were travelers. He expected us to tell our story.

Tanya began explaining in detail and the conversation went well. She told him what we were doing and how we had gotten here and how long we had been at it and what places we had come through and he loved all of it.

I was listening, but mostly watching the horse.

It was a marble-gray draft horse big as four horses. It was the biggest horse I had ever seen. Hooves huge as plates, legs like pillars, neck thicker than the trunk of a thick tree and a noble trim head.

The horse was near us in the field with the father's two sons. One boy was scything the hay in rhythmic swings. Sun gleamed off the blade. The other son was on the horse; the loins of the horse were so vast his legs stuck straight out. A travois, lashed together from young birch trees, was harnessed to the horse.

The horse and the two sons were working together, cutting hay and transporting it to a haystack. They were all sweating. It was a smooth operation. All three seemed to enjoy it.

"Mark!" Tanya was speaking to me. I spun my head.

"He wants me to ask you what you are thinking."

The father was looking at me. It was hard not to look at him when he did this. His mustache was luxurious, his eyes gay. He handed me another chunk of bread and the cup of tea.

"I think it is the greatest horse I have ever seen."

Tanya translated this, then laughed.

"He says, 'Yes it *is* the greatest horse you have ever seen.' "

"It is so heavy," I said.

Tanya repeated this and the father nodded his head.

He was sitting cross-legged and twirling the ends of his mustache. He was looking at me. The sun had somehow come down closer and it was warm. His wife was napping on her stool. The air was calm and the canvas broad and everyone but Tanya had fallen asleep.

He began speaking only to me. Tanya translated slowly.

"You have traveled much."

"Some," I said.

"Many countries, no?"

"Yes."

"But you have never seen a horse like this."

"No. Not like this."

He nodded as if this were something he already knew.

"It is my horse. Someday it will be my sons' horse. This horse is called *Svabodny.*"

"Where did it come from?"

He grinned. He waited for a moment and let me look out at the horse again. The horse stood waiting. Monolithic. It was hard to understand how big it was.

"It is a story . . ." he paused. "It was during the war. That is where all stories begin in this country."

I smiled but he did not.

"I was a boy. Almost a man but a boy still. My mother and father had died. My brothers had died. I set out to walk away. I had nothing. I walked."

He stopped. He was looking down at his hands.

"One day I came to a farm. The farm was empty. I could tell it had been empty for many days. That horse was in the barn." He pointed.

"I was small. I pulled myself up on him and rode away. I wanted to ride away from everything. I rode at night. Svabodny and I, we worked during the days and rode during the nights. Always east. I heard there was nothing there. That is what I wanted, nothing. So I rode. Rode and rode.

"I saw terrible things and kept riding. Many months I kept riding. Then I reached this valley and stopped."

I had said nothing.

"Do you understand this story?" His face had changed. He was smiling.

"I think so."

He stood up and beckoned his sons. They unfastened the travois, pulled up onto the horse together and thundered over to us.

The sons slid down and shook my hand. They shook Tanya's hand. The others had been awakened by the ground shaking so they shook their hands also. Then the boys stood by their father.

The horse waited. Still and magnificent and unbelievable. Colossal. I could see the veins thick as thick rope on its stomach. I could see its eyes calm and waiting and its huge nostrils expanding and its heavily muscled back dripping with sweat.

"*Yezditye verkhom.*"

I looked at the father. He was looking at me.

I stepped forward, reached up, took hold of the mane with both hands, and leapt on. I came clear up, far above the earth.

I took the reins and we rode together. We rode across the mountain valley under the sky and I could feel his immense weight and the heat of his greatness and his giant heart thudding up through me.

24

"N<small>ATASHA</small>!"

It is days later. I'm standing in a meadow by the river, bellowing. The sky is disemboweled by trees on the ridge. Rain is washing the mud off my legs.

We have found there are villages on the river. The river is called the Shilka. Every day we ride west taking game trails through the wilderness between the villages.

Last night before the rain when the river was black and too silent for its size and our campfire was the only light left on earth.

"Think you're going the wrong way," Tom said. He knew she was.

"No I'm not." The tape on her handlebars had come off. It was the third time. She was spiraling it on backward, again.

"You need to start at the bottom and wind up." Tom had told her this each time before.

"I know."

"But you're not doing it. You're going the wrong way."

Natasha refused to answer.

Hands take a pounding bicycling all day. When your handlebar tape comes off you lose the little padding you need to keep them from going numb. Your hands go numb and you can't steer.

"Natasha, I can't spare any more tape."

Tom carries a small roll of duct tape in his repair kit. It is indispensable. We need it to repair tent poles, bicycle pumps, panniers, pedals, seams, shoes, blisters, cuts. When Natasha's handlebar tape slips off again she will ask Tom for the duct tape to patch it back on, and Tom will give her some.

This morning we were wending up a trail on a rock shelf above the river. The trail was dangerous because it had begun to rain. It was slippery. You could look over sideways and see the water far below.

The trail ended unexpectedly on a precipice where the river had torn off the side of the mountain. We hauled our bikes up into the trees. At the crest we found a game trail that went through the forest along the edge of the mountain. We bicycled quietly in the drizzle, pine needles sticking to our tires.

After a few hours the trail dropped into a large meadow beside the river. The meadow was completely sealed off. On the left was the massive river, on the right, mountains. A side stream coming down from a cleft in the mountains cut the meadow in two. It was an insignificant stream but a coniferous jungle had grown up around it. Our trail turned right at this barrier, away from the Shilka, and moved toward the mountains. It slowly twined into the side-stream thicket and led to a hut.

The hut was covered with moss. The door to the hut was four feet high. When we rode up I half expected elves with wild fox snouts and pointed ears to step out. But it was empty. On a shelf inside we found bowls woven from strips of birch bark.

Fyodor rode back out to the center of the meadow. The hut was a dead end. He was searching for a path that kept paralleling the Shilka. The villagers had told us that no matter what, to someday get out, we had to follow the Shilka.

We heard Fyodor whistle and began riding back to the meadow. Natasha had to stop. Weeds and mud had wound up so tight in her cogs the rear wheel was immobilized. We rode around her.

Soon as Fyodor saw us, he bicycled away, diagonaling down close to the Shilka. He had discovered a route across the side stream. Everyone followed him. I stopped to wait for Natasha.

Several weeks ago at night.

"Think you got them upside down," Tom said. He knew she did.

"No I don't." Natasha was trying to repair the headset on her bicycle. She had it apart in the birch leaves in the firelight.

The headset is part of the steering mechanism of a bicycle. It is what the handlebars slip down into.

"You've got the ball bearing cage upside down. Your handlebars will barely turn if you put it back together like that."

"I know."

"But you don't because you've got them upside down. You can ruin your bike that way."

She refused to answer.

"NAA TAAA SHAAA!"

My voice is drowned by the water in the air.

"God damnit Natasha."

Everyone has long since vanished following Fyodor.

"You should be here by now."

I wait a little longer.

"You're taking a leak."

I wait. Rain drums on my shoulders. I notice my ankles and hands are light blue. My neck is stiff.

"C'mon."

Noting where the others went out of sight, I ride back toward the hut. I keep expecting to see her coming my way. I slide into the coppice and find the hut. She's not there.

I search for clues and discover a barely recognizable path. It is a path used only by animals. It leads from the hut up the eerie stream into the cleft in the unknown mountains. I am certain she could not have gone in this direction. I ride back out to the field thinking perhaps she has cut down and somehow gotten ahead of me. I'm hoping. I find the spot where everyone disappeared and follow their trail through the tangled brush into the second meadow.

Tom and Torie and Tanya have stopped. I run my bike
toward them. Through the rain, I can just make out Fyodor
and Pavel. They are riding on.

"Where's Natasha?!"

"We thought she was with you."

"She's not here?" I can hear the panic in my voice.

At the beginning of the trip Natasha bicycled with her head
down. I suggested she look up once in a while.

"I do!" She feigned shock.

"I mean maybe lift your head and see your country."

Tanya was translating so I knew the conversation was
doomed.

"I do!"

"But you don't. You don't even know where you are going."

Tanya shrugged her shoulders and wouldn't translate anymore.

At lunch we were all sitting beside the road eating and
Natasha rode right past. She didn't see us. She didn't hear us
shouting at her. Her head was down and her back curled as if
it were a race.

"NA-TASH-A!?" We scream together and throw our arms
up in the rain to get the brothers' attention. They stop. They
look over their shoulders for a long time before reluctantly
turning around and riding back.

We decide. Tom, Pavel, Torie and Tanya will ride on along
the Shilka to the next village—wherever it is, however far it
is—and wait there. Fyodor and I will go back to the first meadow
and search for Natasha. I know he's hoping what I'm hoping—
she'll be there, waiting.

She isn't. We ride to the middle of the meadow howling her
name. Over two hours have passed now.

When we reach the hut we make a token search but we already know. There is only one place she could have gone. It is
a place so dark we don't want to follow her.

"Ana svinaya idiyot!" Fyodor says. She is a fucking idiot.

The path is obscure and creeps through the copse into the
mountains. We lose it and find it and lose it again. We crash and
shove through horned bushes and vines and trees with roots

like snakes. Sometimes we can ride. Sometimes we must push. Sometimes we crawl.

We move for over an hour searching for mud. We are going mad searching for mud because we haven't found one tire track. Not one footprint. The trail is so tentacled and indistinct and wicked we're thinking Christ maybe she didn't go up here fuck maybe we're wrong, maybe.

It is still pouring when we reach an ominous clearing. We find a bank of mud along the stream, and there they are: two crisscrossing lines all alone. The tracks go down into the water and come up on the other side.

"*Ana svinaya sumashedshaya.*" She is fucking mad.

What I want to believe is this: Sometime Natasha must stop and realize there are no tracks in the mud, so we can't be ahead of her. Then somewhere inside everything must click and she will know she is going the wrong way.

I stand in the rain staring at the tracks and realize even then she will not stop. Natasha is Soviet.

Once, before the Shilka and before the railroad tracks and before the swamp, Natasha said to Tanya:

"He talks too much. He can't just *do* it. He likes to lie there and talk about life and religion and philosophy. It's bullshit."

I don't know why she told Tanya this. Perhaps it was in an extraordinarily rare moment of gentleness between them.

This was a few nights after Tom and I were drinking vodka with the windows of the hotel room wide open. We were on the fourth floor sitting on the windowsill. It was a hot damp dark East Asia night in Blagoveshchensk. It was three in the morning and we were shirtless and sweaty and drunk.

"Have a look." Tom pointed down into the square.

Natasha was walking away briskly. She was walking alone in a blouse so sheer her breasts even from that far up in that kind of damp darkness could be seen bouncing. We had never before seen her in high heels.

A day later the sound man for Carl's film crew was bragging in his innuendo way. He was the only one who wore fashionable clothes. He was suave. He looked as though he should be from France rather than the USSR.

A day after that Natasha said, "At least my boyfriend is a communist."

But it didn't last. She told Tanya he talked too much after they did it and sometimes even before and worse he liked to talk philosophy. And religion! Natasha hated intellectuals.

Farther on we cross the stream and find her tracks again. They go cutting down through the mud into the creek then the water is deep and . . .

We stop. Both of us in the current in the rain holding our bikes. We see the same thing and think exactly the same thing and our heads snap reflexively side to side and our eyes scan the dense brush around us and above us and behind us and quick again and again.

We see her footprints beside the tire tracks going up the mud on the far bank, and beside her footprints, other prints. Each print is so large it is a hole. The holes are staggered and sunk in the mud. They move lazily but neatly alongside Natasha's child-size footprints.

Fyodor looks at me. "*Pyidyatina.*" Cunt.

We move on but slow now. Very slow. We are listening. Watching.

The next time we cross the stream, it is the same: the tire tracks, her footprints and right beside them, the big tracks. I stoop to spread my hand inside a print and stick my fingers in the claw marks. A shiver goes up my spine and I jerk up and whip my head around and Fyodor is standing there swinging his head around too and we both know the animal knows we are here.

We move on. We are hunting. Again.

We cross the stream several more times before the valley starts to widen. Around a bend we see what we cannot believe, a cabin. It is set in the notch of a hill. Beside the cabin is a hayfield. In the field are three men. They see us but do not look up and do not stop cutting until we get close.

"Looking for the girl?"

Fyodor asks them when they saw her.

"Maybe three four hours ago. Rode right by. We yelled and she didn't hear us and she was just right there where you are. She just kept riding."

"See the bear?"

"No bear."

"Where's the path go?" Fyodor points up the valley. Amazingly, there is now a muddy path that winds down from the notch in the hill, dips around the cabin, and turns up the valley.

"*Balota.*" All the men smile.

The tall one points to a dilapidated motorcycle and sidecar beside the cabin. It is rusty with strands of wire sticking out as if someone had started to take it apart and then quit. I try to imagine how they got it here. I try to imagine how *they* got here.

"Want to look?"

The man drops his scythe, goes to the motorcycle, throws his leg over and starts it with one kick. Fyodor leaves his bike with me. He steps into the sidecar and they groan away.

Three weeks ago beside a campfire insignificant in the morning rain, Natasha called Tanya a *shalava*, a whore.

They seldom ever spoke to each other. When they did they argued maliciously, usually for less than a minute.

"He wouldn't believe in it now, if He saw it, if He lived here now." Tanya was revolted. She had dumped her bowl of *manka* into the grass.

Manka is wheat meal. We had gotten it the night before in a village store. The store had had nothing but wheat meal and champagne. They wouldn't let us buy champagne.

At first we thought the black lumps floating in the cereal were chaff from the wheat. We were hungry. We ate most of it before realizing, almost simultaneously, that the lumps were rat feces.

"Yes He would. It had to be this way," Natasha said.

"He said it was going the wrong way right before He died."

"You're lying." Natasha looked as if she would hit Tanya.

"No, He did. Just before He died He wrote many long letters renouncing all of it but they have kept them secret." Tanya knew things like this.

"You don't know a thing." Natasha was devout.

"Things are not better, He would see that." Tanya was a heretic. Natasha believed she should be burned.

"What things? Things are much better." Natasha was screeching.

"For some."

"Not for the whores!?"

"Not for ordinary people." I could see Tanya was giving in. She was weak. Natasha had limitless contempt for weakness.

"You mean not for the capitalists and the whores."

"Not for the people in the villages."

"They have food!"

The two haymakers let me sit on their straw mattress in the hut out of the rain. It is dim inside. They try talking to me for a while. They want to know where I have come from. They give me a stale hunk of bread and a jar of homemade blackberry jam and go back to work in the rain.

I wait twenty minutes. Half an hour. An hour. I retrieve my journal from a pannier and start writing.

I can see Natasha. She is pedaling and pedaling and pedaling, blind. I can see the bear. The bear is patient.

Two hours. Three hours. I write this whole story in my journal lying in the haymakers' hut.

It is growing dark and still raining when I hear the groaning and come out just as they pull up. Natasha is in the sidecar. She is unapologetic and unchanged, her smooth young face calm.

I realize Natasha is a parable.

25

FYODOR, NATASHA AND I made it back to the Shilka before dark, then followed the lines in the mud in the rain along the black river. At midnight we rode into camp. Pavel was asleep but Tom, Torie and Tanya were waiting, huddled around the campfire with their hoods up.

Natasha said nothing. Her chin stuck out like wood and her eyes were wood. She ate the smoking bowl of boiled potatoes Torie handed her then went to her tent. I told the story.

Fyodor slumped down by the fire. He wouldn't eat. He stared at the wet flames with his head hung between his knees. He looked poisoned. His cheeks and nose and forehead were green, as if he'd been hit in the face with a shovel. He had been scared.

Not for himself—of the thousand fears inside every human, fear for yourself is a small one. If the only fear you must face is fear for yourself, the only pain you must endure your own pain, then for the love of God life is simple. You can steel yourself or lie to yourself or blow hard pride into yourself. You can stand straight up and forget your own mortality and be loose and liquidy, drunk on your own fear and resolve, and do something someone will someday call brave.

Fyodor had not felt that lucky fear.

There is only one fear that slices you all over inside as if you

153

had swallowed a scalpel: the fear for *another* human. Take someone you love, your child or brother or mother, and imagine
them being hurt. That is fear. Fear you don't know where to
find the courage for. Fear you cannot get drunk on.

In the morning nothing was said and Natasha never said
sorry but it was all forgiven. There was no other way. The seven
of us had to eat and sleep and ride together. We would be in
each other's faces, and in each other's blood and shit and
dreams. So you cough it up before it chokes you.

We broke camp and rode through another river village. It
was still raining and the streets were deep in mud.

"The mayor was the one who invited us in," Torie said. The
four of them had spent the evening in the village bakery.

"It was so hot inside," Torie said, "that drippy hot with the
windows foggy. The floor was so warm we took our shoes off
and walked around barefoot."

"Really." Something inside my left leg was hurting. It had
been hurting for a few days but I'd ignored it. Now it was
throbbing and I was feeling queasy and couldn't say much.

"The mayor stuffed us with fresh bread. Right out of the
ovens with hunks of butter. Can you believe it? My whole body
finally got warm."

"Trying to imagine it."

"She said the bakery makes bread for all the villages on the
river. They deliver it by boat in the summer."

"Huh."

"I thought about you guys, eating the bread with my feet
sweating, out there in the rain." Torie looked over and smiled.

"Bet you did."

We were ahead of everyone. We could see the moving gray
water between the cabins. It made me sick to look at it. I tried
to concentrate on our conversation.

"Bread. That's great. Your mayor say anything about a
road?"

"Why yes," Torie laughed. "In fact she said her husband was
a truck driver. She said we were quite near the road and that
her husband drove the bread truck in the winter."

The notion of a road was a joke by now. Or a riddle. A
Siberian riddle. If we wanted to make each other laugh we'd tell
a story about some mad homunculus we'd met in a river village

who said the road was only over the next mountain or around
the next river bend or just right here under our wheels and we
were on it. We called it Siberian existentialism: Wherever you
go there you are, probably—wherever you are there you go,
almost.

We reached the end of the village. The cabins and the road
stopped. Ahead, a pasture ran along the bank until the forest
came down from the mountains and pushed it into the water.

Torie jerked her head like a mare and leapt up into the
pasture.

"Truck driver in the winter huh," I yelled weakly. I was so
giddy my bike seemed to want to throw me.

"On the road," Torie said over her shoulder, pointing to the
water.

It was hard for me to make our lunch stop. When we sat
down beside the trail I was dizzy. I put my head back against a
tree.

We were on top of a mountain in a stand of tall birch. Perfect
straight armless birch. They seemed so white to me. Lumines-
cent. I decided they were waiting for winter, like saints waiting
for the consecration. Brilliant holy falling and layering white on
white to cover up the messiness because summer was like a
hunchback or an ogre with carbuncles who must be painfully
lanced and then smothered under a white sheet and secreted
out and buried and . . .

"You don't look any better than you did last night." Torie
was sitting beside me. She was talking to me. "Funny color."

"Don't feel so fine," I said.

"Why?"

I was looking up. I noticed a few trees already had yellow
leaves.

"Is it August yet?"

"Cut the coy act."

"My leg just hurts. You can have a look at a lump if you
want." Immediately I wished I'd said nothing.

"A lump?" Torie scooted over. She loved this kind of thing.
Lumps and bumps and bizarre infirmities. I lifted my left leg.
She gasped.

"Why didn't you say something?"

"Thought it was just a bug bite at first."

"Yeah right. How long have you had it?"

"Few days." She bent over, held up my leg and looked at it closely.

"Jesus Christ Mark, it's big as an egg. Tom, come here." Her voice was shrill.

Tom came over and had a look. I looked at my leg with them. Just below my left knee on the outside of my upper calf was a hard shiny red lump. The skin was stretched out and deformed.

"Prehistoric cuckoo birds," Tom said definitively. "Big fuckers looks like." He turned his head sideways. "Yep, that's what's in there. Wings like bats, teeth like needles. They're incubating."

I tried to laugh. Tom touched it.

"Damn it Mark. It's hot as an iron. Are you taking antibiotics? Torie?" But she was already disgorging her panniers searching for the medical kit. She returned looking grim as a nurse.

"Four a day for five days. Do it."

I couldn't believe a bump in my leg could hurt so much. I couldn't believe it was making me so sick. I said something like that to Tom.

"All prehistoric cuckoo birds incubate in volcanoes like that," he said. "It's gotta hurt." He went on with a long imaginative story that would normally have had me rolling.

After that everything fades in and out. In my head sequences and events and pieces of time float, rising and falling and rising again in the dark like sparks from a campfire.

From the beginning in Moscow I had been writing in my journal every night, usually two pages a night. There are only two words for the next six days. They sprawl across the page in a script I cannot recognize

I remember the trail turns into a path and we pass milk cows big as elephants and a cowboy on a horse with a tail like an

alligator and gallop into a village people all around and I'm
worrying I have the red bird-egg bump on my face and we are
inside a schoolhouse and there is a painting of Him hanging
above me that scares me and someone is looking down at me
staring at my leg and I am asleep and they say while I'm dreaming trying to make myself well

iz *balota* iz *balota* in a whirly voice

and hospital and road and I laugh to myself and then try to
wake up and say no fucking hospital I'm fine but I don't have
a language so I keep lying there on my side in a cold sweat on
the planks with His eyes down on me like hot irons under the
ocean and swim to the surface and explain it's nothing really
really and tell everyone to stop it stop worrying and laugh at a
hospital and laugh at a road cut that coy shit

when we're riding at dawn in curly white mist like giant feath-
ers with some kind of desperateness and Torie asking me if I'm
sure I'm all right and I say of course in someone else's voice
then someone is yelling after us yelling the road is just around
the next mountain and everyone laughs even me but my laugh
sounds high and silly like someone else's someone tricky and
evil using my voice and pretending to have my face while I have
to concentrate my brain searing concentrating on the pain because it is impossible to do anything else.

Now I remember I was lying in the grass and everyone was
asking if I was OK even Natasha and I always said yeah yeah
sure because I should be tough and I can barely hear my own
voice which isn't mine and I stare at my big lump and now my
ankles are thick and greasy and filled with liquid and Tom
makes jokes that any day they will have to fledge and the prehistoric cuckoo birds going cuckoooo cuckoooo like in my head
at night will fly out gnashing their teeth and the wound will
close up like a vagina and everything will be fine and I always
say yeah yeah right right because I like the story and it keeps
me going.

Then the clouds are gone and it is just Tom and I riding
ahead up and up through the trees and Tom is staying close to
me because I can hear him breathing and the end of a road
appears up high high up in the blue sky and it is brown and
graded and graveled and we pop up easily like two corks coming up from the bottom of the ocean and Tom has thrown his

bike down jumping down up down Mark Mark Mark damn it we did it we did it we did it we

but my mind is sky is leg is swimming streaking like a slippery finger painting I made when I was five me my red bike because I am my leg fucking piece of shit leg but I won't look because the skin is the wrong color so we just wait till they are all there rejoicing hugging each other saying we have done it done what no one believed we could do fuckers said was impossible so fuck fuck fuck all of them over and over all together we did it we did it we did it.

Then there is a day I remember clearly when we rode and rode on this road going away and everyone was happy. Even the Soviets were like this and I thought all of you are fools don't you know anything because I knew better I knew the *balota* was all around us like elves and satyrs and they would come for us any minute and everyone was once in a while still asking me Can you make it Mark Hey Mark Hey Mark can you make it and I'm saying sure no problem really no problem trying not to show it while I'm melting burning frying in my head just trying to stay in the saddle is everything concentrating so unbelievably hard and not talking at all and when I do talking with this other voice letting everyone know it's no big deal really even though by now my whole leg is swollen like a bloated animal and what you can't see under my shirt what I don't want anyone to see is my abdomen swollen hard too.

Then we reach a village on the road and it is the one the man in the schoolhouse talked about when I was sleeping and this picture snaps into focus as if I'm looking at somebody's life going on down there through binoculars. Everything razor sharp.

I see the hospital is a log cabin. There are men in torn shitted pajamas wandering dribbling in the dirt outside the hospital. A woman comes down the wood steps. She is clean and attractive even though she is wearing a tall white puffed-up hat that only a chef would wear or a doctor in Siberia. But she is not a doctor. She explains this. She explains that there are no doctors here. I am draped in cold sweat and burning with a bloated leg and hardbucket belly and she makes me put on a clean white smock all my reeking clothes still on underneath and escorts me up the stairs into the cabin through a hanging canvas curtain into a room.

In the room there is a birthing chair with outstretched metal claws and old blood on the sheet and rags and tissue covered with new blood and pus and phlegm in a wastebasket.

"I'm sorry," she says, "there is no running water."

She is very pretty in her chef's hat. I realize she is not a nurse either. She is a woman told to run the hospital and the hospital has nothing and she just cares for people who must see someone before dying or becoming crippled or going mad.

She is delicate and looks at my leg. "I have seen this before. It is from the swamp."

I tell her what must be done. I try very hard and make my voice my own voice so she won't think I am not brave.

"*Nyet!*" Her voice is trembling. I understand. She is too afraid.

She washes my leg with alcohol that feels cool as ice and then finds in a metal cupboard a small jar of gray mud and covers the swelling with slimy paste. The smell is putrid. It is swamp mud. She has put on swamp mud to heal what the swamp gave me and there is something in this I know but I can't think of it.

"This will help," she says, and I know it won't and smile.

Then she wraps clean white gauze around and around. She tears the gauze and ties a knot over the swelling and I flinch and we are finished.

"That should do," she says

I walk down out of the hospital trying not to limp and she pats me on the back and I am alert and understand it is a placebo and ride for several hours in the afternoon under the sun trying to believe it will work not thinking about what I already know I must do until a snap of voltage begins to explode every time my abdomen touches my thigh and I think perhaps tomorrow I will be a cripple and it will be impossible for me to ride and that cannot happen.

We make camp beside a pasture just inside the birch where the sun is running straight in lighting up the leaves and making the trees glow and keeping me warm in my cold sweat while I keep trying to set up my tent but it takes a long time. It seems complicated. I make one move at a time. And rest. And move again and rest. I lay my bag in the middle of the tent and get in and zip up the door and stare at the mosquitoes trying to get in at me. I touch my groin and feel the glands under the skin protruding like walnuts. I work hard on the little big fear, trying to steel myself.

After a while I crawl out and go to Tom and Torie's tent. I ask Torie for the medical kit.

"Mark."

I don't answer.

"Mark." Torie grabs my arm. "Don't do it."

I find the razor in the medical kit and go back to my tent. Someone has used it. There is hair and soap on the blade. I clamp the blade in my pliers and limp over to the fire and hold the blade in the flames. The hairs and soap sizzle and burn black.

I get back to my tent. I sit straight and feel the sweat hot and cold and hot and cold and feel loose and tense and scared and drunk with fear and going away in my head but concentrating very hard. I unwrap the gauze and wipe away the dark paste. I hold my leg down with one hand and steady the blade in the pliers over the mound of flesh. I move slowly without shaking and cut deep and blood and gray matter and pus spray across my hand and my leg and I lie back.

26

I T IS HOT in my tent when I open my eyes. I unzip my sleeping bag and sit up. I feel fine and can't understand why it feels so strange to feel fine. Warm light is coming through the top of my tent. I look at my watch. It's after eleven. Suddenly I jerk back my sleeping bag.

Thick brownish scum has dried in puddles under my leg. It smells. The swelling is down. A gruesome scab has formed over the cut.

I flop backward and lie still on my back with my hands under my head.

"YESSS!" My own voice has returned.

"Let the cuckoo birds out, huh." Tom is kneeling beside my tent looking in through the mosquito netting. He is smiling. He is quite calm.

Everyone has been packed for hours. Tom and Torie help me load my bike and we push through the pasture up onto blacktop.

Then I'm riding. Sliding. Gliding.

"It's a road," I whisper. The sound flutters away with the wind. "A *road!*"

Tom is riding right next to me. I realize he has been riding close beside me for many days.

"Tried to tell you that two days ago."

I fall back through a webbed fog. I see everyone jumping down and up and down on a gravel road in the sky.

Tom and I. We just pedal together down the highway.

Torie wheels up and Tanya and then it's the four of us sailing over the blacktop above the earth. Both women keep staring over at me.

"What?!"

They look back down the road and begin to laugh.

After a while it's just Tom and I again. The girls have dropped back and are riding alone together. They are chattering. The Soviets have disappeared ahead of us pounding hard as they can with their heads down.

We're floating through farm country. Fields and pastures and barns. I feel as if I've been away for a long time.

"Seven hundred and eighty-nine," Tom says.

We start a hill and it goes so smooth and easy. I can feel the blood and pus spurting from my leg and running down into my shoe and it hurts and it feels wonderful.

"What was that Tom?"

We bank along the top and there are no fences and I can see the black ribbon going over and over every green hill until finally disappearing. I feel as if I'm in a painting. Not an Impressionist painting. A Grant Wood.

"Remember the little girl on the big bike? Where the road ended?"

I nod.

"From there to where this road started two days ago, was seven hundred eighty-nine miles."

The day after that the press and the rumplesuits and Carl with his film crew find us. They zoom up over the asphalt. They are joyous. We are back on the map, back in the Soviet Union.

The next day, August 2, in the evening in a gloamy orange haze, we bicycle into Chita.

PART THREE

27

Hot showers first time in a month. Then sleep. Sleeping.

Sleeping till the sun through the hotel window makes you sweat your sheets but you keep lying there fabricating fantastic hot morning dreams because you know you don't have to ride today and that can make you so frisky you could wake yourself up but you don't you just stay swaddled in your own hot safe wet sleep.

Up to your feet finally. Showering again. Long long scalding showering till your skin's boiled and your muscles soft as stringy balloons and the steam's so thick you're breathing it like opium. Step out dripping and sweating and flop naked into a chair. Drink Chinese beer. Then the steam has come out and wet the ceiling and the chair has printed your ass and you walk back into the bathroom and startle yourself in the mirror because you're somebody different. Thin. Face dark as a damn piece of wood. You shave to make it better. Doesn't. The person you thought you were won't come back.

Go barefoot sneaking down the hotel hall to the buffet, eat something, go back to your room. Don't wanna see anybody.

Sleeping.

Hear a knock at night. "Grease and spanners are by the door." Tom don't wanna see nobody either. Nobody wants to see nobody.

Now look at your bike in the glossy moonlight. Walk over lift it up and spin the wheels. Spin the pedals. Crunch the brakes. It's bad. It made it and it was steely and immortal but now it's bad.

You crack open the door and pull in the bucket of grease and the big wrenches and a cardboard box. This will be good. Drink another beer.

Lay her down. Wheels off. Chain off. Pedals off, like undressing a woman. Taking your time because that's the only way. Hubs and headset and bottom bracket undone and stripped off and scattered all over the floor.

Rags? You need rags. Pop the pillowcases.

Then fingers deep in that moonlit grease. Lubrication. One orifice at a time. Wiping the inside walls clean until they gleam.

But some things are shot. Made of metal and still worn down. Need new shiny silver balls new chain new freewheel new derailleur pulleys new chainrings, but you have them all right there in the cardboard box because they're exactly what you thought would wear out and you'd put them down on that first napkin as if they really were all you would need.

Sleeping.

Sleeping on the floor with the blanket pulled off the bed and the moonlight on your face and on your bike sleeping by you like a dog.

Wake up early after the moon but before the sun. Shower again just for the hell of it. Then back to your bike.

Wrap on the slick chain plug in those pretty pulleys tighten down the chainrings and douche the whole beautiful veteran mama with the blood of oil until it drips onto the carpet. Then take her for a spin down the hall.

Pick up the new black tires leaning against your door and snap them on her like a dress and tweak this and tweak that and go riding down the hall again this time so smooth and soundless you're almost invisible but not quite because the floor lady sees you and wags her finger and you laugh and she shouts so you roll back into your room and fall off into bed and into sleep and wake up writing in your journal and then, finally, go out for a walk.

*   *   *

Chita is a big city. Industrial with buses and shops. I toured the downtown until I found a bookstore. Him everywhere, the selection limited to His political treatises, Dostoyevsky, and maps—all the same map, just different sizes. I bought a big one and went back to the hotel.

I spread it out on the bed and found Chita. On the map it didn't look like a big city. It was shoved clear over in Asia, just a little pinched dot two hundred miles north of Mongolia and maybe two thousand miles south of the Arctic Ocean and what looked like a good five thousand miles east of someplace called Leningrad.

I beat on the wall above the bed and yelled.

"Hey Thomas. We've come a third."

The wall thudded back. "Next stop: Lake Baikal."

I didn't see the Soviets or Tanya for three days. They too had vanished in the folds of the hotel.

The night before we left, Torie and I met in Tom's room. He had the windows thrown open. It was a warm night. He was still tinkering with his bike because he'd spent the first two days working on Tanya's. He was sitting on the floor in his shorts. We were happy to see each other again.

"I spoke to Carl." Tom stood up and passed out sweating beers.

"What's he been up to?" Torie fell into a chair. She was relaxed. She sat sideways with her feet crossed.

"He's filming all kinds of crazy stuff. Siberian fire fighters, bus drivers, village scenes. He said he plans to catch us on the road every few weeks. He's arranged for the supply truck to meet us in the big cities." Tom handed me a list. I read it out loud.

"Irkutsk, Krasnoyarsk, Novosibirsk, Omsk, Chelyabinsk, Moscow . . ."

"He'll make sure we have a hotel or hot shower at each one."

"That's good of him," said Torie.

"You know what else he said?" Tom paused. "They lost us in the swamp. All of them. The cops. The KGB."

"Maybe they finally realized bicyclists aren't a security risk," I said.

"Maybe . . ." Tom was grinning ear to ear.

"What's so funny?"

"This morning I had a meeting with Carl and some big-shot police chief from Moscow."

"What!?"

"We have to sign papers that say they're not responsible for us."

"That's it? No more cops?"

"That's it."

We clacked our beer bottles.

"But . . ." Tom grinned, "they said we won't make it. They said the road's bad and there's no food."

We all started laughing.

"We're free," I whispered.

Tom shrugged. "We'll see."

28

In the morning the police escorted us out of Chita, and stopped, and we rode west, bound for Lake Baikal. Infamous Lake Baikal, the deepest lake in the world.

At first it was cold and foggy. We moved over the swales and swells like little sailboats, barely able to see each other. By afternoon it was raining.

It rained for three days. The dark water shrunk our heads and turned our necks to stakes and stiffened our knees. It burned our hands blue and blanched our lips and puckered our genitals. The landscape was habited and furry with forests but it all seemed savage to us because we were freezing.

We rode village to village and foraged and found food. We found enough to keep going. We were used to it. The villagers, they were used to it.

In the country a woman stood on the side of the road with a bucket. We bought the bucket and crouched eating the strawberries in the cold rain till we all got stomachaches.

In the village the *stalovaya* was closed. A woman saw us peering through the window. She was warm, splayed and smoking. The sign said open. The door was locked. The woman saw us and laughed so we could hear her through the streaming glass. She blew smoke rings.

In the village there was a cement building with a small cage

window. There was a crowd around the window with a thick
line coming out into the street. It looked like a giant rat with a
long gray tail, the snout and teeth and claws shoved through
the hole in the building. Men were hitting each other.

"What are they waiting for?" asked Tanya. We were swoosh-
ing through the dark water together.

"I don't know."

"You should know. By now you should know."

"I don't know."

We swooshed back into the forest.

"Vodka."

In the next village the bakery had no bread and the grocery
no food. The *stalovaya* was closed but a woman saw us peering
through the window and unlocked the door and quickly herded
us in and locked the door behind us and we were inside out of
the rain getting warm and she fed us steaming beef stew with
napkins and touched our faces and slipped us back outside and
locked the door behind her and waved through the streaming
glass.

A 92-mile day a 101-mile day a 71-mile day. Each night we
camped in the ditchy wet woods and each tenebrous morning
coaxed a fire from the rain.

One day we rode up to the outskirts of Ulan-Uda. We could
see it from across a bend in the Selenga River. Miles of tenements and medieval factories and black smokestacks. We took a
bridge over the river away from the city.

We were cold and hungry and our heads were puttied, but by
now we knew better. Visit one Soviet city and you know everything you ever wanted to know about the Soviet Union. And
nothing about Russia.

When we reached Lake Baikal it was still raining. The water
was rough and black. Not one of us cheered or ran down the
shore. We did not shake hands. Lake Baikal had been a big
goal—one of those dream places from childhood—so we should
have felt heroic, but we'd been cold for three days.

No one ever tells you this but the hero feeling is pretty weak.
Most any kind of normal pain will knock it out of you. Cold,
heat, hunger, ear infection, bad gas. Indeed the hero feeling
usually only exists after the fact. It slinks out hours or weeks or
years later when the undeniable honesty of pain has dissolved

and you're warm and happy and have a drink in your hand and a drunk tongue in your head and lies are lighting up everyone's eyes.

We pedaled into an empty village scattered up the shore. Rainy cottages, mud streets, pieces of pasture and the black tits of storm clouds flattening down on all of it. We found a grocery store and crowded inside. It had shovels and nails and sacks of wheat with mice feces and rope and tins of fish that gave you worms. The proprietor was stuffbellied and dry inside his dry store. We were shivering. He said the next store was many miles down the lake. A cigarette flopped in his mouth. We asked if he knew someone in the village who could sell us anything to eat. He didn't answer. He was drunk. We went back into the rain.

Fyodor was staring at the lake. Heavy black water rushing against the shore bouncing the little sailboats. His face was old and his fingers were bent and blue as if they'd been broken. He was shaking.

"*Maya strana balnaya.*" My country is ill.

It was the first time Fyodor had said anything about his country. It was the only time. He took off down the road along the lake and Pavel and Natasha followed him.

They were out of sight when a woman appeared in the rain on a bluff in the village. She wore a blue raincoat with a pointed, habitlike hood. A large pail hung from one hand. Her other hand was cupped up to her face covering her nose as if she were weeping, or laughing. Rain was coming down on her. She stood very still staring down into the black water as if she could see under it.

Tanya ran out to her. They were in silence on the bluff in the blacktitted clouds, then they linked arms and walked back down.

"*Kartofli!*" Tanya shouted joyfully.

The woman had a beautiful round head. Her cheekbones were red balls. She stood with the pail in her hand and looked at us. Her eyelashes were blond and straight and her brown eyes unwavering. I had no idea how old she was. Perhaps she was thirty, perhaps sixty.

She held out a pail. I was shocked she could hold it out with one arm. She kept her other hand in her pocket. There were enormous red potatoes in the pail. They were muddy and glistened in the rain.

We wanted to buy half the bucket. She would sell only the whole bucket. She showed us the potatoes with her thick fingers.

I knew she lived near this village beside the deepest lake on earth. She had risen at five in the morning and hoed her garden. She had risen at five and planted her seeds. She had risen early every morning to make her potatoes grow and this morning dug them up and walked to town and stood waiting all day in the rain for three rubles.

Tom gave her three rubles. Torie loaded half the potatoes, one at a time, into plastic sacks. She left the rest in the bucket.

"It is food," the woman cried.

"It is too heavy," Tanya said.

The woman shook her head.

"It is too heavy for us to carry," Tanya said.

The woman nodded abruptly and stepped back onto the edge of the bluff. It was still raining.

A motorcycle with sidecar came around a cottage. There was a man with a beret in the seat and wooden rakes strapped with rope over the sidecar. The machine was the color of a salamander. The engine clucked and the wheels kicked and the machine shuddered into the grass beside the woman.

The woman lifted her raincoat, pushed the rakes aside, and stepped into the sidecar. She sat down holding the pail in her lap, turned to us, and smiled.

I looked out at the water. It was so immense it seemed to me to be an ocean not a lake. I was staring at it trying to see what she saw, trying to see underneath. I couldn't do it very well. Perhaps I was too cold. I saw mostly the rough black surface.

I packed my bag of potatoes on my bike and waved at the woman. She had been watching me watch the sea.

She waved back. Then she stood up and stepped out of the sidecar. She left the pail on the seat and walked over to me. She came up so close I could look into her eyes if I wanted. She did not blink.

She lifted a fist from her pocket and held it steady in front of me. With her other hand she caught my wrist and turned my palm up. Rain fell into my hand. She opened her fist over my hand, dropped something into my palm and closed my fingers. It was something so weightless I could not feel it in my palm. She pushed my hand up to my face and opened my fingers. A delicateness, wet and warm, fell against my nose. Over the blur of my thumb and fingers I could see her face. She was smiling. She had lifted her own hand over her nose to show me. Then she walked back to the sidecar.

I breathed deep. The aroma slipped up through my nostrils into my head. It filled my head. It was strong and sweet and damp and warm. It was mint. A gift. My bike God.

29

SOMETIMES YOU MEET someone you know.

You have spent nights together. Night upon night for years talking and talking. You have camped together beneath the sky and sung songs together and drunk beer in each other's homes. You have hugged and cried and laughed together. And you have never met.

There are few such people, but they are the ones you will always know and who will always know you. They are in parts of the world where you haven't been. They are living lives you cannot know. They have sisters you have never met whom you've danced with on the porch and brothers you cannot see whom you've wrestled in the grass. They have kitchens with bright windows you can't imagine, where you had coffee a thousand times. These are the people you meet, and know, before you speak.

I met Saulius Kunigenas and five other Lithuanians in the trees beside Lake Baikal. It was raining and we were cold and we saw the smoke and wheeled off the road over the wet leaves up to their campfire.

We shook hands and hugged each other tightly. They were kin. They were our blood. Bicyclists. Nomads. They immediately shared their lunch and we shared our potatoes and stories filled us.

The Soviets did not exchange a word with any of them, and after eating, rode away.

The Lithuanians had bicycled together thousands of miles through many countries: Estonia, Lithuania and Latvia, Georgia and Armenia and the Ukraine, Kazakstan and Tadzhikstan and Uzbekistan and Moldavia. They had ridden their terrible pot-metal bicycles everywhere they were allowed to travel. This was the first time they had come to Russia.

"Why?" I asked Saulius. We were riding side by side now along the deepest lake in the world.

"Because this is not a country. Have you not noticed?" Saulius's nose was curved and handsome as a beak. His eyes bore through everything they fell upon.

"Then why have you come here?"

He did not answer.

Then we traded bicycles. Me on his heavy clanking machine, he on my light strong steed. We arced together above Lake Baikal. The road was absolutely perfect.

Saulius let my bicycle take him. I saw he understood how to fly my bike. He let the bicycle take him until he was smiling and winging and diving and I was on his bike grinding hopelessly and he was flying, hooting like an owl, as if it were a miracle and he was a boy again.

Suddenly he stopped pedaling and waited for me to catch up.

"I have come here because I lost a part of my wife beside this lake."

Saulius looked over at me. He was floating freely on my bicycle. He saw I was trying, as best I could, to ride his bike.

So he told me the story.

This man was not tall. His back was curved with muscle and his chest gray with wiry hair. He was on a straw mattress sleeping hard after seventy years. He was working his farm through the night, blood booming under the hide of his forearms, fingers twitching. He had worked his farm since he could walk. He had raised five children.

His youngest son had stayed. He would be a farmer. He was tall and bony and freckled with ears that stuck out like cardboard flaps. He was twenty. He lay very still, as if knocked out, his red hair ruffled to one side. He could not work all night yet.

A daughter was home visiting. She slept in her old room at the back of the cabin where she and her sisters had grown up together whispering and giggling. Her dark hair lay across the pillow. Her face was pale, the veins of her temples like faint blue cobwebs. She was tired. She had shown her two children her life on the farm all day. In the high sunny fields and in the hay in the barn and chasing chickens and riding their grandfather's giant horse. She was a young, strong, elegant woman. Her children were small, the little boy two, his older sister three. They were all together in her bed as she had been with her older sisters. Fast asleep.

It was spring. The night carried a strong sweet damp smell from the pasture. It came in through the window.

The old man owned the farm. Sixty-seven acres trim as a backyard. He had worked it by himself all his life. He raised wheat one year and corn the next. Let this or that piece of land lie fallow and poke up with jack pines where he could get a deer in a bad year. Sold eggs and sometimes a chicken, goats, every spring almost half the sheep. Cursed even around the grandchildren when he cut himself. Smelled like the barn except on Sundays.

It was a cool farm night and he was sleeping hard, building an irrigation ditch by hand with a shovel.

The daughter visited often. She wanted her children to see how her father worked. How he loved to work. She knew they were young, but he was suddenly, as if in a breath, old. And she wanted to talk to her brother. Tell him to forget and be quiet and please just forget because he would sometimes go to the village and someone would overhear him speaking his mind and that made her stomach fall and keep falling until she could not eat. But most of all, she wanted to sleep her own sleep inside the farm. The nights were always cool and the stars would sing to her children and she would sleep dreamlessly and breathe deep the smell of her hope.

That spring something came into her sleep. She did not wake, but her father was already up, his trousers undone, his hands still around the invisible shovel as if it were a weapon. It was his farm and he could hear the squirrels sleeping in its far corner.

He knew how his pigs snored and what his giant horse said at night. This was not his horse.

They were coming slow. Too slow, trying to be quiet.

He put on his boots and a shirt he'd pressed himself and stepped across the room to his son's bed. His son was awake.

"Soviets," the boy whispered. He spoke in Lithuanian. It was May 22, 1948.

"Wake Ada. Dress the children warmly. Take him out the back of the stable. All four of you ride together. Take the hill path along the trees to the far cottage. Cross the road to Second Pasture. Cross Three Fields. Go to Königsberg."

"Königsberg? It's fifty miles."

"You make it by breakfast."

The son had never heard his father's voice like this. He stepped into his pants and went quickly to the back room. He touched Ada's hair and she opened her eyes. The little boy woke and began babbling. He was asleep. Palmira, the little girl, she would not wake up. The son was trying to be gentle but Palmira began to cry. The mother put her hand over Palmira's mouth but Palmira was still half-asleep and frightened and began to scream as if she were in a nightmare.

The horse began to gallop. The grandfather ran back through the cabin and shouted whispering Get out! Get out! Get out! hoarse and quiet and desperate and there was whinnying and voices and the front door shuckled and burst open and they could not run or think or speak and the grandfather stood up and walked too fast toward them and they used a rifle butt and tore out his mustache and his front teeth and two more held a rifle against the throat of the son and lifted him off his feet by his neck against the wall until he was choking and turning white and the mother held her children under her arm and bit the tip of her tongue off.

They were put on the horse cart, the grandfather's unconscious head cracking against the wood and the son dazed and pale and cut in the neck and the mother holding her children. It was far in the night and the stars were so quiet. When she looked up she began to cry. And her children cried in the night and the soldiers were ashamed and so laughed louder.

They were taken to a train station. It was still not light. Low across the cobblestone there were hundreds like them, and dark men using their rifle butts. Once a light came on in a window in a house by the square, and then snapped off.

They spent a month on the train in a freezing burning cattle car. There were tears and more tears and blood drying and then vomiting and humiliation and hiding and human excrement.

They were taken to the shore of the deepest lake in the world. They were told they would spend the rest of their lives there. They were told they would build a road around the lake.

They lived in the forest in barracks. The brother and grandfather were sent to a camp where they broke rocks with sledgehammers for the bed of the road. The mother logged. She used an ax and cut a path through the timber. Early in the morning and late at night she cooked on a fire.

Once Palmira was limp and round-eyed and burning with fever. The mother carried Palmira through the night through the snow nine miles to ask the commandant for permission to go to Irkutsk for a doctor. He said no. She carried Palmira back and by then it was morning and she had to march to work. She was weak and saw she could die very quietly just letting her heart stop and closing her eyes and sinking into the snow.

In 1957 Khrushchev let them return to Lithuania.

"So I have come here," Saulius said.

We were still above Lake Baikal on the perfect road.

"But the camp must be gone by now."

"Perhaps."

"What could you do if you found it?"

"I will walk where she walked with her mother. Palmira is my wife. I will bicycle to this place and stop and walk in the woods."

We camped together that night. After dinner, Saulius and I walked along the shore of the lake. It had stopped raining.

"Mark. On July 21, 1941, Lithuania was annexed by the Soviet Union." Saulius was speaking slowly. He was looking out over the water.

"We had been a sovereign nation for hundreds of years. We were older than Russia. We were a country as advanced and progressive as Finland . . . we have our own language. We have our own alphabet. Your alphabet, the Roman alphabet.

"From that day on, our children were forced to speak Soviet in school. I was forced to speak Soviet. Speaking our own language, even outside class, was prohibited.

"On June 14, 1941, deportation began. Schoolteachers, university professors, ministers, doctors, engineers, architects, writers, artists, religious figures. And their families. Forty thousand people vanished in the first three months. Most were never heard from or seen again."

We kept walking along the shore. We could hear the dark water.

"Deportations continued through the war. In 1946 deportation of farmers and their families began, and the rapes, and murders, and . . ."

Saulius could no longer speak.

The next morning it was raining and mud had washed over the earth and Saulius and I had spent our lives together.

We tried to say good-bye. Not a word would come out.

He rode one direction down the lake and I another. He upon his horrid bike and I upon my lucky one. I tried to ride my bike the way Saulius had ridden it, but I couldn't.

I turned around and waved and he was waving at me. Then I dropped my hand into my pocket and felt the piece of paper with his address and rubbed the mint in my fingers.

30

IT IS RUGGED, beautiful country around the southern end of Lake Baikal. Heavily timbered mountains rise right out of the water. The road is like glass. The road is absolutely perfect.

Irkutsk lies on the west shore set deep in a long inlet. We reached it in two days and checked into a hotel. Tom and I asked for separate rooms but were told there were no extra rooms available. They said the hotel had been booked for weeks, so we shared a room. It was small and narrow with two bowlegged beds along each wall. We brought our bikes up in the elevator.

The rain had washed the grease from Tom's left pedal making it click like a cricket. My bottom bracket was grinding. We decided to spend the day overhauling our bicycles. Tom went to the buffet and returned with a knot-muscled chicken. I went out on the street for beer. When I got back Tom was in the bathroom.

"You tried this yet?" He was yelling through the door.

"What'd you expect?"

"Awkward as hell. Somebody wanted the whole affair to be as uncomfortable as possible."

This was not an old hotel. From the outside it appeared to be like any other Soviet hotel, and it was in the comical ways—no toilet paper and no soap, spitefully crooked bathroom tile, hot water only on occasion. But, in fact, this hotel was unique. All the toilets in all the rooms on all the floors had been set in the corner of the bathroom, facing the wall, so you couldn't get your legs in and had to sit twisted sideways.

We drank and ate and worked on our bicycles all afternoon. We didn't talk much. We liked the work. The sun heated our bottles of beer and made the cramped room sweaty and pungent. We used the hotel towels for rags and the two shoe brushes to scrub the mud off our frames.

"What we need is a refrigerator," Tom said. His face was dripping.

"Why?"

"Bad beer would be better cold."

"None of the rooms have refrigerators, I already asked."

"They always say that."

"Bad beer is like bad intentions, temperature doesn't matter," I said.

"What're you? Mark the fucking-philosopher-bike-mechanic?"

By dark we'd finished our bikes and the beer. We stood our steeds up at the end of our beds, lay down with our stained fingers clasped on our chests, and stared at the ceiling waiting for the moon.

"Tom . . ."

"Yeah."

"There must have been snitches everywhere."

"Must have been." Tom began to whistle. It was an old war tune. He whistled slowly. The notes drifted through the room like bubbles.

"I mean everywhere. The churches, the stores, the schools. A whole hideous world of snitches."

"Yeah."

"Did you see Saulius's face? God, the hatred."

"I know."

Our eyes were the only light spots left in the room. We were talking wearily with big gaps. Night air was coming in through the window.

"Christ. Who could you trust? Who could you speak plainly to?"

"Your family. Your friends."

"Where?"

"I don't know. The walls have ears."

"The ears have walls."

"Maybe. Maybe." Tom stopped whistling.

"It's not like that now."

"You believe that? Or you want to believe that?" said Tom.

"I don't know."

"Tanya told me something. She said this is the only country where dissidents don't want to change the system. She said, 'It is too evil. They just want to leave. They pray to leave.'"

"You know what Saulius said? Have you noticed there aren't any men in the villages?"

"Yes."

"Between World War II and Stalin, fifty million people were killed. *Fifty million*. Lithuanians, Armenians, Russians, anybody."

We stared into the dark for a long quiet spell. We were falling asleep.

"Tom, do you like it here?"

"I like being here very much."

In the morning there was a note for Tom under the door. There was a room available. He walked downstairs to the reception desk. The clerk handed him a key and said nothing.

I helped him pack his gear and we took it down the hall to his new room. I pushed his bike and he carried his panniers and sleeping bag.

He had trouble unlocking the door. The key didn't fit right. We'd had the same struggle with door locks everywhere in the Soviet Union. It was as if the manufacturer had intentionally designed the lock to make the door difficult to open, but easy to shut.

It took Tom a long time. Finally. We carried his gear in and dumped it on the bed. I rolled his bike against the wall.

Tom walked over to the window to pull the drapes because the room was hot and stuffy. He stopped halfway, turned around and smiled. Then he set the hotel key on top of the refrigerator and popped open the drapes.

31

"Com'er you. Com'on you little ratty ratrat." Tom was squatting on the highway. He had his arm outstretched and a crust of bread in his hand.

"Look at 'im! Scared as can be."

We were surrounded by mist and meadows and falling down fences, three days west of Irkutsk, two days east of Krasnoyarsk. Tom was practically sitting in the middle of the road.

"Nope, don't trust you guys. Nope nope nope." The voice was animated, low and burbly like kid farts underwater.

The dog had watery eyes and broken ears. It was trotting away, stopping, looking back. It was a small street dog, obsequious enduring eatdirt dog. Tail tucked up against its belly, ribs showing.

"Oh, I don't know. Just really don't know." The creature had stopped on the far side of the road, its body turned away but its head twisted back.

"Com'er you little ratdog. C'mon fella." Tom was still on his haunches. He gently waved the bread.

"Oh oh oh. Don't try to fool me. I've been kicked you know. Kicked kicked kicked. So I know. I know I know I know." The dog looked at Tom with that forlorn downworn dog look. It didn't bark. Ratdogs couldn't bark. Their voices had been kicked out.

"OK," Tom was disheartened, "that's the way you feel . . ." He stood up and began walking back.

"All right all right all right. But I'm late. I'm late I'm late I'm late." The dog had lowered its head and begun treading bravely forward, eyes on the bread dangling from Tom's hand.

"Aren't as scared as you thought, are you, you little ratty ratdog." Tom stopped, growled mockingly, then knelt down, his back still toward the animal.

"Nope nope nope. Not at all. You guys are all right." The dog sniffed the crust, cowering, then snatched it and quick-footed away.

We were all sitting on the guardrail. Tom looked at Fyodor.

"Got a lot of them here," Tom said.

That night we were invited by a village mayor to camp in the school gym. It was an extraordinary log gymnasium. Two full basketball courts end to end, both painted Easter-egg green, an enormous hardleather vaulting horse, ropes, ladder rungs, and seven mattresses—one for each of us. We spread out, each in our own space.

After several hours Fyodor invited me to his mattress. I sat down in a cube of warm, syrupy light. Particles of dust rose slowly and drifted about our heads like tiny stars.

"*Klyuchevskaya Sopka,*" Fyodor said, his bristly face almost touching mine. He had drawn a mountain in the back of his journal. It looked like a volcano.

"*Kamchatka!*" He seized his pencil.

The Kamchatka Peninsula is a sword of land in Eastern Siberia. It drops south through the Pacific Ocean cleaving the Sea of Okhotsk from the Bering Sea. It is serrated by the Sredinnyy Mountains. The highest mountain in this range is Klyuchevskaya Sopka, a remote icy peak poking 15,500 feet above the sea. Fyodor wanted to climb this peak, with me.

Scribbling ferociously, he showed how he could arrange to have a military helicopter fly us to the base of the mountain and how they could fly in the equipment and supplies as well and how some unknown number of previous attempts had failed and how so many Soviets had died and how he and I (he plugged his chest and then mine in the starspangled luminescence), being strong, being *men,* could be the first, the conquerors. He drew many pictures of exuberant misery—icicles hundreds of feet high, avalanches, storms, unimaginable Siberian cold.

This was expedition talk. It was the only way Fyodor and I ever communicated. I too had never finished a trip without the back of my journal crammed with notes for the next one.

There is something about long journeys. You're lucky if you manage one in a lifetime, and by the time you're done you're swearing *by God never* I'll never do it again. But then some evening, months or years later, while you're browsing through the atlas, whistling or humming or eating, whop! A few weeks later you're gone. And if you somehow find yourself on just one more good long journey, something gets in you, like a worm gone up through your feet. From then on, somewhere inside every unbearable trip (because there will always be another trip), you'll swear up and down *this is it dammit God damnit this is it, period*. But then you'll find your way back to your own warm bed and clean bathroom and beautiful world and discover they're just as they were when you left, and after another month or two or six, this thing inside you will start to swell and throb. You'll become restless and sore as if your bed were too soft and your bathroom too bright and suddenly your beautiful world has again grown moldy with mediocrity. So you'll pull out the atlas and fall into it and the next morning buy an airplane ticket and just when everyone thought you were finally figuring it out, you're gone.

Fyodor had it bad. He would die of it. He had told me he spent less than three months a year at home. He had a wife and three children.

"Kamchatka?" I said. I wasn't really listening. The light was purple now, stirring a galaxy of tiny planets as if it were liquid.

"*Kaneshna, da!*" Fyodor said. Yes, of course.

Fyodor hadn't noticed the light. He couldn't, he wasn't here. He was never here. There was no here-and-now for Fyodor. No present. His life was in the future. Right now he was climbing Peak Klyushchevskaya on the Kamchatka Peninsula above the ice-filled Sea of Okhotsk. When he was climbing on Kamchatka he would be skiing to the North Pole. When he was skiing to the North Pole he would be sailing around the world.

"*Mozhit byt'*," I said. Maybe.

"*Mozhit byt', pochymu? Klyuchevskaya gara—muzhchinskaya gara.*" Maybe, why? Klyuchevskaya man's mountain.

I didn't want to tell him yet. Trip talk was our only talk. Without it we would have nothing to say to each other.

"*My dalzhni sdyelat' !*" Fyodor said. We must do it.

Fyodor believed he and I had the same disease. We didn't. We had the same symptoms but different worms inside us. I went to be. Fyodor went to be done.

"*My dalzhni?*" I said. We must?

"*Kaneshna, da!*"

At dawn the mayor walked us through her dusty village to the *stalovaya*. There was a surprise waiting for us.

"Pancakes!" Torie was ecstatic.

Breakfast was Torie's favorite meal. Cups of burning black coffee and pancakes piled a floppy foot high. She believed in breakfast.

The *stalovaya* was inexplicably immaculate, the windows clean and the tile floor shining in the yellow morning light. There were freshly cut flowers in vases on the rickety tables. The village hadn't seen coffee for months, but the pancakes, wide and glowing and smoking hot with globs of fresh jam, were here. Torie was euphoric. We sat down and dove in.

"Lord. If we could only have this every morning," she said. "Tomorrow and the day after tomorrow. All the tomorrows." She thrust out her tongue and flicked up a dribble of syrup going down her chin.

"I would like that," I said.

"*Zaftra.*" Torie whispered. "*Zzzaaafftrrraa.* That is a wonderful word for tomorrow."

Natasha abruptly broke in.

"*Nyet, tol'ka sivodnya.*" No, only today.

"What?" I said.

"No pincakes tomorrow," Natasha said. I couldn't believe she was speaking English.

"Why?" I said.

Natasha reverted to Soviet and Tanya began translating.

"It is wasteful to think of tomorrow," Natasha said.

"Why?"

"We are here today. We are only here today."

"So what. So you can't have hope for tomorrow?"

Torie was watching the conversation. She was eating her pancakes. I was speaking for her and she knew it and the yellow light and huge pancakes and clean walls were all around us and she wouldn't let anything spoil it.

"No, only today."

Pavel was sitting next to Natasha. He looked blank and uninspired.

"What does that mean?" I asked.

"Tomorrow is only tomorrow and it will come and you cannot change it," said Natasha.

"Then you never think of tomorrow, Natasha?"

"I wait for tomorrow. I see only today." Natasha stopped talking and shrugged her shoulders as if it were obvious I was an idiot.

You know, Natasha, you *can't* see only today. Today is the slipperiest thing imaginable. It's invisible. Look at it and it disappears. You can only *be* the present, you can't see it. Trying to see the present is like trying to watch yourself blink in the mirror. You only see the present when it's dried, like the emulsion of a photograph or the ink on a page, dried and died and become the past.

Tanya suddenly looked up as if she'd heard me.

"Mark," she was smiling. "Do you know that there is no present tense for the verb 'to be' in our language? You cannot say 'I am' or 'she is' or 'you are.' In Russian, 'to be' is only in the past, or in the future."

Natasha scowled at me confidently, then spoke.

"*Tol'ka sivodnya.*"

Tanya and I rode together that afternoon. I had to be careful riding with Tanya. She still didn't know how to ride. Her bike remained an enigma to her. She had wrecked over ten times.

Once she tried turning too sharply, flew over her handlebars and slid violently through the gravel. She tore the skin off her left shoulder and gashed her elbow to the bone. She was in shock and needed stitches. The town we were near didn't have a hospital. Torie stanched the bleeding and was able to close the wound with butterfly bandages from our medical kit.

On another occasion Tanya somehow tipped over on wet

pavement and knocked herself out. She was lying in the middle of the road and a bus was coming. Tom and I barely pulled her onto the shoulder.

It was as if Tanya were drunk or drugged whenever she got on her bicycle. Off the bike, she could find food in barren villages and interpret convoluted conversations and evaluate the most suffocating emotions. But Tanya and I rode together often because she always had a story.

"I will tell you about when I went to America," she said.

"Please."

"I am not from a rich family. We have money, that is all. Money is nothing in this country."

I didn't believe her. She'd told me before that she flew to the Baltic countries for vacations several times a year. She'd told me she always somehow avoided the month of potato planting mandatory for all students at the Institute of Architecture. She was from a rich family. She was not from a family who were members of the Communist party. That is what she meant.

"Last year I went to the airport in Moscow in November. I had my ticket. I had got the ticket in May. You must buy a ticket for America one year ahead of time. My ticket was for May the next year, this year."

Tanya liked to tell me stories but she could not tell them around the campfire or in a *stalovaya*. Natasha or Fyodor or Pavel would scowl her mouth shut for her. If she continued they would shout, "*Shut up* Tanya. He doesn't need to know that." Sometimes Fyodor would threaten to beat her.

"I wore an expensive dress. A dress of silk, very low in front. And perfume." She turned to me and ran her finger down between her breasts.

"Watch the road," I yelled. We almost caught handlebars. She was quiet for a moment, consciously trying to steer a straight course.

"You could see my legs. I had my hair up and wore diamond earrings. I wanted to go to America very bad. I brought only a purse. No suitcases.

"I went to the office of the airport boss. The airport boss said it was impossible. 'Your ticket is for next year, not for today,' he shouted. 'No, no, no,' he shouted.

"I pleaded. I cried. I was wearing an expensive dress and

leaned so he could see under my dress. He was a monster. He was a hairy monster. 'Impossible. Impossible. Impossible,' he said.

"I walked very close to him. I took off my diamond earrings slowly. I held them tight in my hand for one moment. My mother had given them to me.

"Then I put the diamond earrings into his hand and flew to America."

I looked over at her and smiled. She smiled back, then went on. There was always more. Sometimes she told it, sometimes she didn't.

"In America I had no diamond earrings. I had no dollars. It was cold in New York. My friend was in L.A. I had to go to L.A. My ticket was still for March. I cried. I spoke in Russian only. I made it to L.A. the same day."

We glided for a while, then she glanced at me.

"You see Mark. Here, in Russia, prices are just higher."

That night all seven of us were around the campfire.

"Torie, what is the name of your other bike? Your bike at home."

She looked up at me and smiled mysteriously, without opening her mouth. I knew she had another bicycle. I didn't know if she had a name for it. I just guessed. All great bicycles have great names.

"A name for a bike . . ." she said hesitantly, "is something special. Like the name of a character in a book. It makes all the difference."

"Yes, I know."

She stared into the fire. "*Dilsey*. That is the name of my road bike back home. Do you know why, Mark?"

"I think so," I said.

Torie waited.

I stared into the fire. " 'Dilsey: They endured.' "

By the time we pulled into Krasnoyarsk, we had each named our bicycle. We found some silver paint and put the words on our frames.

Tom named his bicycle *Blagarodnaya Sabaka*. Noble Dog.

Fyodor named his *Kaneshna, Da!* Of Course, Yes.

Torie named hers *Zaftra*. Tomorrow.
Natasha named hers *Tol'ka Sivodnya*. Only Today.
Tanya named hers *Moy Monster*. My Monster.
Pavel named his *Vdakhnovyeniye*. Inspiration.
And me, I named my bicycle *Svabodny*. Free.

32

WE STAYED IN the monolithic Krasnoyarsk Hotel. It was dim
and unexplorable. We were the first Americans ever in Krasnoyarsk—it had been a closed city for seventy-two years—so a
reporter appeared in the morning.

Tom and Torie and I sat on a broken couch in the lobby. The
reporter was dusty, his glasses thick and opaque. I believed he
could not actually see us. He drummed a blunt pencil on his
notepad and began asking questions through his translator.

The translator was tall and lean as a cane. He wore a clean
suit coat and tie. He looked like the kind of man who had
always worn a clean suit coat and tie. His name was Alexander
Tarasov, Sasha.

Sasha had been listening illegally to VOA and the BBC since
he was a boy. He had read every scrap of English he could find.
Inside his long, gaunt head was a confused library of black
market American novels and illicit radio reports and twisted
government monologues. Sasha had been waiting patiently and
solemnly, for three decades, to meet an American. He grimaced
translating the reporter's questions.

"How do you like the Krasnoyarsk Hotel?"

We nodded. We were still tired after a long night of sleep.

"It is the biggest hotel in Siberia."

"Ah, *bal'shoy*," I said.

"*Da, bal'shoy!*" shouted the reporter. "*Vy gavaritye pa-ruski?*"

"*Nyet*," I said. "I just know what the word *bal'shoy* means."

The reporter was perplexed. Sasha translated for him. The reporter began scribbling in his notepad.

"Do you know, my American friends," Sasha looked down at us, "Mother Russia *has* created the biggest microchip."

We laughed. Sasha looked over his black glasses and tried to let himself smile.

"I am so sorry. This reporter is an ass."

"It's all right," Tom said.

"May I ask you a question?"

We didn't know it yet, but curiosity was leaping and banging inside Sasha like a grasshopper in a jar.

"Sure," I said.

He caught his breath. "Do all Americans own airplanes?"

Before we could answer he was off and running.

"Do all Americans carry guns is it true that young people actually own cars is it true that anyone can buy meat anytime they want is it true that American streets are filled with garbage is it true that there is no military draft and no rationing and . . . ?"

His questions came so fast he ran out of air and had to stop. The reporter stared at him with a blank, walrus look, put his notepad in his pocket, and left.

We took turns answering Sasha's questions. Our answers disturbed him. The picture didn't match the one he'd painted in his head.

"I see it is not what I thought," he said. "I should have known."

"Nor is Siberia, for us," I said.

Sasha allowed himself to smile, sorrowfully.

We talked for over three hours. Then Tom and Torie excused themselves. They wanted a nap. Sasha asked me to lunch.

"We shall go to the nicest restaurant in Krasnoyarsk," he said.

I shook my head. I wasn't up for a restaurant.

"Please," he said, "I am a Russian. I know how to do it."

The doorman stood in front of the glass doors. His shoulders were wired inside a moldy suit coat. His hair was ribbed with grease. He had a cigarette in a gap between two teeth.

"Hello," said Sasha.

The doorman stood in front of the doors, hands in his pockets.

"Excuse us," said Sasha.

The doorman didn't move.

"Excuse us," said Sasha.

"The restaurant is closed," said the doorman.

Sasha peered over him at the sign on the door: OPEN 1:00 P.M. TO 10:00 P.M.

Sasha looked at his watch. The doorman's eyes narrowed. His pockets bumped like snakes in a bag.

"It is two P.M.," Sasha said politely.

"The restaurant is closed," said the doorman.

"Oh, the restaurant is closed?" said Sasha.

"Yes, the restaurant is closed."

"Why is the restaurant closed?"

"It is closed because it is closed," said the doorman. His hands sprang from his pockets and clutched the handles on the glass doors. He grinned. His teeth were pointed. Smoke leaked from his nostrils.

"When will the restaurant open?"

"Can't you read!" the doorman shouted. Sasha looked at the sign.

"Yes, I can read," said Sasha.

"The restaurant is closed." The doorman tilted his head like a rodent. He had a sharp nose and black oily eyes.

"I would like to speak with the manager."

"There is no manager."

"In that case, I will speak to the hotel manager." We turned to go.

The doorman's cigarette had now burned down to his teeth. He spit it out and stepped away from the door. We went inside.

It was a cavernous hall. The lights were off and the drapes pulled. The maître d' sat behind a desk. He was extraordinarily fat. He was leaning sideways whispering into the stiff blue hair of a waitress. The waitress, vastly buxom in an open blouse, was leaning just far enough forward. She had one painted pink eye toward us and there was glitter imbedded in her blush. She looked like a carnivorous fish.

"Could we please be seated?" said Sasha.

We waited.

"Excuse me, could we please be seated?"

The maître d' pulled his face from the blue hair. The waitress reared back shaking her breasts. She spun her hair around and fishtailed heavily away. Her skirt was short and her nylons had runs going up between her legs.

The maître d' looked through us. His eyes were puffy. He had a large pale face for his head and a large head for his neck. His hands, large and red, lay palms down on the desk like two small pigs on their stomachs.

"Could we be seated," said Sasha. "A table for two, please."

The waitress swam back and pushed out her monstrous breasts. She had brilliant pink fingernails sprouting from her white hands. Her hands looked like dead rabbits. She laid one on the desk and one on her hip. She seemed to be trying to look inside the maître d's ear from four feet away. The maître d' was still looking past us.

"You are the maître d', are you not?" said Sasha. "Could we please be seated?"

The maître d' stared through us. The waitress stared into his ear.

We waited.

"Excuse me. Could we please be seated?" said Sasha. He spoke politely, as if we'd just walked in.

The maître d' turned to the waitress and pulled her forward with one of his red pigs and stuck his nose into her blue hair. She bent out over the table with her dead rabbit hands spread apart, and winked at us.

We waited.

Sometime later the maître d' groaned and yanked his head out of the waitress' hair. She jiggled herself up and swam away.

"Take any table." He had glitter stuck to his lips. He coughed and something came up in his mouth and he began chewing.

About half the tables were occupied. In the center of each table was an identical Matrioshka doll. People were eating silently or waiting and talking or waiting and not talking and waiting. Sasha and I sat down at a small table.

We waited. No one came to our table. We looked back at the maître d'. He smiled. We waited. Sasha called over a waiter.

"I am not your waiter," the waiter said nicely. He had his

hands gripped on a round platter. They were green and looked like lizards.

"Who is our waiter?" asked Sasha.

"Your table is not being served," said the waiter.

"Why is our table not being served?" asked Sasha.

"Because the table you are sitting at is not being served, I am sorry."

"I see. I would like to speak to the manager." Sasha smiled.

"I am sorry, I am not your waiter," said the waiter and he went away.

The manager never came. Sasha waved over the waiter again.

"I would like to see the manager," said Sasha. The waiter nodded. "I am not your waiter," he said and left with his lizards clinging to the platter.

Sasha pulled over a different waiter.

"I would like to see the manager," he said. This waiter popped his head back and forth like a pigeon and flew away. Sasha smiled at me.

When this second waiter again flittered by, Sasha grabbed his arm and reeled him in like a flapping pigeon with a hook through its beak.

"Please bring us the manager."

Some time later a large woman in a green metal dress rolled up to our table.

"Hello," Sasha said politely.

"Hello," she said back. Her lips were pale green.

Sasha spread his fingers over the tablecloth.

"Is this tablecloth the same as the tablecloth on that table?" Sasha pointed to an empty table next to us.

"Yes," she said.

"How about this doll?" Sasha touched the round, serene-faced Matrioshka doll. "Is it the same as the doll on that table?"

"Oh, yes."

Sasha picked up his fork. He twirled it between his fingers. He let the handle fall into his palm and with a flick of his wrist dropped the prongs of the fork onto his plate. He shrieked the fork across the plate.

"Is this fork the same as the forks on that table?"

The woman had enjoyed the sound Sasha made on the plate. Sasha looked up at her and pushed his fist forward shrieking the fork across the plate again. She smiled enthusiastically. He was pleasing her. She swung her head like a turret.

"Yes, they are the same. Everything here is the same."

"We would like two menus, please," said Sasha.

The woman undid her arms and pulled two menus from underneath her armpit. Her hands were round and humped. They looked like turtles. The menus were wet from being under her armpit.

"This table is not being served," she said. "I will send a waiter."

Sasha and I chose from the menu. We waited and a waiter never came. Sasha called over the first waiter.

"I am sorry. I am not your waiter." He was smiling desperately.

"Could you please tell whoever is our waiter, we are waiting and we are ready to order." Sasha spoke tonelessly, one hand pinching the waiter's collarbone.

"Your table is not being served," said the waiter and jerked away.

When the chance came, Sasha reached out to grab the second waiter winging by but this time the fellow dodged him, beating his black elbows and shrieking angrily, "I am not your waiter!"

Sasha began to get up. Just then the woman came back. She rolled over to our table with a pen and notepad clutched in her headless turtles.

"What would you like to have?" She was smiling.

We ordered. She wrote it down and rolled away.

We waited and talked. We waited and talked and our food did not come.

Sasha hailed the waiter who was not our waiter and told him to bring the manager and then shoved him away before he could say anything. The manager came.

"Our food has not come," Sasha said politely.

"Who did you give your order to?"

"You took our order."

"This table is not being served. You must sit here." She plunked a turtle on the table next to us. We moved to it. She smiled and said, "I will send a waitress."

"We are now at a different table," Sasha shouted to the waiter not our waiter.

"I am not your waiter," the waiter winced.

We waited. We watched everyone else waiting. Some time later a waitress appeared. She was the buxom carnivorous one. I noticed now she had gold teeth and a pleasant smile. She leaned far over our table just for us. She thumped her dead-rabbit hands down on the tablecloth. We gave her our order.

"You can't have that." She shook her head of high blue hair. The glitter on her cheeks sparkled like scales.

Sasha pointed to the item on the menu.

"That is not possible," she said.

We made another choice from the menu.

"That is not possible," she said, smiling. I could smell her torn nylons and her breasts.

"What is possible?" said Sasha.

"Beef Stroganoff and soup with sour cream." It was not on the menu.

"We would like that very much," Sasha said.

She swam over to the maître d's desk. We looked at her and she winked and raised her ass in the air for us. Some time later she went into the kitchen and brought out two small plates of sliced cucumbers.

"Excuse me, where is the soup?" Sasha said.

"There is no soup."

"There was supposed to be soup."

"Who did you talk to?"

"You."

She smiled her gold teeth.

"Is there salad dressing?" Sasha asked.

"There is no salad dressing, only sour cream."

"Could we please have sour cream with our cucumbers?"

"There is no sour cream."

"You just said there was sour cream."

"The sour cream is for the soup."

"But there is no soup."

"Yes."

"Thank you," Sasha said. We began our cucumbers. They weren't bad.

When she returned we had finished our cucumbers. She stacked our plates and walked away. She spent some time squirming at the maître d's desk, then went into the kitchen and came out with two bowls of soup. Cabbage soup. She set the bowls in front of us. In each bowl, floating on top, was a large blob of sour cream.

The soup was excellent. When the beef Stroganoff came, the meat was cold and the grease clotted. We weren't finished when she came back for our plates. She took them anyway. Sasha ordered tea.

She brought the bill. It was six rubles and seventy kopeks. The tea was on the bill. She did not bring the tea. I gave her a ten-ruble note and she swam away. She never returned.

It was after five so we left. The maître d' smiled beautifully as we walked by. He waved his little pink pigs. The waitress winked and waved her bleeding rabbits. The doorman seemed to have been waiting for us the entire time. He smiled graciously and opened the door.

Tanya came to my room that night. She brought hard rolls and beer. We were to attempt a phone call to the United States. She made herself comfortable on the bed. She looked more appropriate on a bed than on a bicycle. She dialed a zero. On the other end the phone rang and rang, then was picked up.

"Hello hello," Tanya yelled. There was no answer.

"Hello hello," Tanya yelled.

The phone hissed, then the line went dead. She dialed again. She tried three more times. She was trying to reach the hotel operator. The hotel operator was in a room two floors below.

"Hello hello," Tanya yelled.

"Yes yes," screeched the voice at the other end. I could hear it from five feet away. It sounded like a bird with its wings being broken.

"I would like to make a call to the U.S."

"You must make a reservation."

"Then I would like to make a reservation."

"You must make a reservation with the international operator, I am the hotel operator." Bzzzzzz.

Tanya dialed again.

"Yes yes."

"I would like to make a call to the U.S."

"I told you," screeched the bird, "you must make a reservation with the international operator."

"Could you please connect me with the Krasnoyarsk operator?" Bzzzzzz.

"I am doing this wrong," Tanya said to me. She bit into a roll.

The next two times Tanya disguised her voice and her Moscow accent and simply asked to be connected with the Krasnoyarsk operator. There was no one else to call. All phone calls went through the Krasnoyarsk Hotel operator. There are no phone books in the Soviet Union.

"Yes." Miraculously, it was the Krasnoyarsk operator. She had the voice of a flatnosed dog.

"Could you please connect me with the international operator?"

"No."

"Please could you connect me with the international operator?"

"No. No international phone calls are made from Krasnoyarsk." Bzzzzzz.

Tanya pulled her hair back and put a beer to her lips. She was lying back on the bed. She tried again.

"Could you please connect me with the international operator?" She had made it through to the Krasnoyarsk operator again and her voice was high from such luck.

"There is no international operator in Krasnoyarsk," said the nasal voice.

"Then could you please connect me with the international operator in Moscow?" Tanya was thinking quick. There was hissing.

"Yes yes yes." It was a shriek through the scratching. It was the international operator. She had a voice like a cat caught in a lawn mower.

"I would like to make a call to the U.S."

"You must make a reservation."

"With whom do I make a reservation?" Tanya felt very lucky.

"With the international operator."

"Are you the international operator?"

"Yes."

"Can I make a reservation with you?"

"No."

"Why?"

"I am the international operator in Moscow."

"With which international operator must I make a reservation?"

"The Krasnoyarsk international operator."

"There is no Krasnoyarsk international operator," said Tanya.

"Yes I know. Krasnoyarsk is a closed city."

"Can I make the reservation with you?"

"I am the international operator in Moscow."

Tanya's voice was controlled. She was allowed to give the number I wanted to call in the U.S. and my room number in the Krasnoyarsk Hotel. The cat said it would call back in one hour.

We waited and talked. Two hours passed.

By some second stroke of extraordinary luck, Tanya made it directly back through to the international operator in Moscow.

"I am waiting for a call back to make a phone call to the U.S."

"Who are you?" shrieked the cat. "Who did you make the reservation with?"

"With you."

"I have no reservation."

"I would like to make a reservation." Tanya went through everything again. The cat said it would call back in one hour.

In one hour the phone did not ring. Tanya again got through.

"I would like to make a reservation to make a call to the U.S."

"Who are you?" Tanya told it who she was.

"You must make a reservation." Tanya calmly made another reservation. It shrieked that it would call my room in one hour. In one hour the phone rang and Tanya answered.

"You want to make a call to the U.S.?"

"Yes."

"But you are in Krasnoyarsk. No?"

"Yes."

"You are making this reservation for an American. No?"

"Yes."

"That is impossible. There are no Americans in Krasnoyarsk." Tanya tried to explain.

"There are no Americans in Krasnoyarsk and there have never been any Americans in Krasnoyarsk so obviously it is impossible to make a reservation to make a call to the U.S. from Krasnoyarsk." Bzzzzzz.

It was the middle of the morning and very dark. We had finished the beers and hard rolls. Tanya was about to leave when my phone rang.

"You were supposed to call to make a reservation," it shrieked.

"Yes, I would like to make a reservation to make a call to the U.S. from the Krasnoyarsk Hotel in Krasnoyarsk for an American."

"Please call in one hour and make a reservation."

One hour later Tanya called. Like a spear she went through the bird and the dog into the cat and made a reservation. Then it told her it was of course impossible to call the U.S. from Krasnoyarsk you had to be an American to call and there were no Americans in the Krasnoyarsk Hotel in Krasnoyarsk because Krasnoyarsk is a closed city so she should call back tomorrow to make a reservation. Bzzzzzz.

I said thank you to Tanya and she left.

Some time later, when I was asleep, the phone rang and far down a hissing line I could hear a voice shouting and I knew it was someone from the U.S. and I shouted back and she couldn't hear me and she said she couldn't hear me and we shouted and shouted and finally both just hung up.

The following evening Sasha invited me to dinner at his home. He did not own a car. He bribed a rumplesuit. We were chauffeured. On the drive across town I told him how Tanya had tried to call the United States. He laughed.

Sasha lived with his girlfriend, Luda, and her mother, in the mother's tiny apartment. When we arrived it was clear Luda and her mother had spent the afternoon preparing dinner for us. Liqueurs and hors d'oeuvres were served immediately.

Luda was a stout woman. She was an English teacher and spoke impeccably. She too had painted an elaborate picture of America.

"We hear so very much about your AIDS. Your AIDS has spread everywhere has it not? Is it not true that one half of the people living in the New York City have AIDS? That was on the radio today."

I tried to explain. She listened intensely.

"We do not believe what we hear. But we do not know," said Luda.

Luda's mother appeared and together they brought out a feast. There were so many elaborate dishes the candles and flowers had to be taken off the table. We ate and conversed about many things. Then Sasha began to speak.

"Well you see, I do not believe you know what it is like here."

"I want to know what it is like here," I said.

Sasha stopped for a moment. No one spoke.

"Well you see. There is this group of people who own everything. This room we are dining in, they own it. This apartment building, they own it. They own the buses and the trains and the boats. And the rivers."

I was watching him. He was angry but controlled. He was watching me.

"I still believe you do not understand me."

I didn't answer.

"Mark, my friend. Let me say it this way." Sasha had eaten little. He was too tall and gaunt to eat. "Everything is *privately* owned in this country. *We* own nothing. Everyone owns nothing.

"Allow me to explain further. These same people, they own the factories and the churches and the schools. Every school. And all the books the children read. They *wrote* the books the children read.

"They own the art and the music. The radio stations and the TV stations and every newspaper and every magazine. And," Sasha's voice was breaking, "they own the language. The bloody language.

"Now. In every newspaper and in every school and in every factory they speak with this language and they say the same thing. What are they saying? We are the greatest country in the world. Every other country in the world is poor and dangerous and ugly and we are the greatest." Sasha had taken off his glasses and closed his eyes. He was weeping.

"Do you understand?"

I nodded.

He shook his head. "No, I'm afraid you can't. You see, if you own the language, you own the people."

I had stopped eating. Luda's mother asked me to please eat.

"There is only one voice in this country and it is not ours. It is none of ours," said Luda. She pointed to Sasha and then to her mother and then to me. Suddenly she seemed to jump subjects.

"Is it true one can buy condoms in a grocery store in America?"

I smiled weakly. Her expression did not change.

"We have just heard this from some friends. It is not true then."

"No, no, it's true," I said.

Luda and Sasha were stunned.

"Condoms are not found here," said Sasha. "They are very, very expensive. One must acquire them on the black market."

"*Other* forms of birth control are also not found here," said Luda, looking at Sasha painfully. She was biting her lip.

I wanted to ask Luda something more, but couldn't. She knew this.

"Abortion. Abortion is the only form of birth control. And the doctors are very poor. And the instruments are very old. Many women are hurt." Luda's voice was falling.

"And of course, sterilization," she whispered. Her face was stricken.

For a long time we all sat at the table together without speaking.

"You see, Mark," Sasha's eyes were still closed, "here, we are pets."

33

THE NIGHT I had dinner with Sasha, Tom was robbed.

He'd gone to Tanya's room and forgotten to lock his door. Tanya and he had talked for perhaps an hour. When he got back to his room all the rubles in his money belt were gone.

It was a small sum of money, less than a hundred dollars. Tom debated telling anyone. Eventually he decided he should report the theft. He called the desk clerk, the clerk called the cops. The rumplesuits came.

Two huge, hogfaced men were stationed outside Tom's door. They took Tom into his room for questioning. They interrogated him for five hours.

When Sasha brought me back to the hotel, there were police everywhere. Sasha was told to wait in the lobby. I ran upstairs. Tom was just being released. He looked dazed and exhausted. His face was gray.

Then they took Tanya into Tom's room. (I was told I would be interviewed in the morning.) She spoke English and knew Tom so she was a prime suspect. They interrogated her for two hours. She came out crying and was escorted to her room.

Then the hogfaced men took Sasha into Tom's room. He had been the first person from Krasnoyarsk to speak to an American so he was also a prime suspect. They interrogated him for many hours. When he was released, around five in the morning, he went straight to Tanya's room. He thought they might have coerced her.

He found Tanya on the floor hysterical and crying and bleeding from the head.

Some time during the night Fyodor had found out about the robbery. He had gone to Tanya's room and forced himself inside and accused her of stealing the money. He had lifted her by the neck and banged her head against the wall.

The rumplesuits never found the thief.

Before we left Krasnoyarsk, Tom and I had a meeting with Fyodor. We tried to explain to him that what he had done was wrong and that we could not continue bicycling with him if he ever touched Tanya again.

"It is unacceptable. You must apologize," Tom said.

Fyodor was offended. He refused to apologize.

"You asshole," I said. "You're way the fuck out of line."

Fyodor's face was blank. He did not understand why we were upset. He said Tanya was a liar and a thief, a whore.

Tom was shaking, the muscles on his chin trembled. "For the love of God! This is only a bicycle ride!"

34

Beyond Krasnoyarsk the wind clubbed us. We had expected it. We were penetrating the West Siberian Plain.

Bound on the east by the Siberian Plateau and on the west by the Ural Mountains, the West Siberian Plain is wider than three Nebraskas placed end to end. North to south it is two thousand miles deep, stretching from the Kara Sea to Kazakhstan. A land disconsolately characterless and flat, it is ravaged day and night by westerlies.

There is only one road that crosses the West Siberian Plain.

For days we didn't lift our heads. Days and days. The monotony was unspeakable, the wind so fierce to move at all was to hunker down into as small a target as possible and punch your pedals until you were exhausted.

One afternoon when the wind had become so malicious we were riding slower than we could walk and our legs and lungs were dumbfounded, we took shelter behind a haystack.

"This is the way geese fly," I said, floating one hand in front of the other. My middle fingers were pointing forward representing two goose necks, my thumbs and little fingers stretched out as wings.

"Together," I said, moving my hands in unison. I flew them in the wind, rising and falling, one behind the other.

Torie was lying on her side, her back warm against my leg. Her eyes were closed. Tom was beside me, and Tanya, beside Tom, was burrowed into the hay. She looked like a mouse peeking from her hole. Natasha was sleeping on the other side of Torie. Pavel and Fyodor were next to Natasha, their backs against the wall of straw.

"I think we should try it." I nodded to my hands flying in formation.

"We tried it before," said Tom. He was writing in his journal.

"I think we should try it again. Seriously this time."

"Funny how you can't see it," Torie said suddenly. Her eyes were still closed. "The invisible juggernaut."

Above my hands I was watching the stands of birch violently bow and crack, rear back and bow again. The field was bucking and smashing. Clouds were wrenching and fleeing. It had been like this for many days.

"I think we should try it again too," Tom said sarcastically. "You want to explain it again?" He smiled blandly and tipped his pen sideways toward the Soviets.

"Maybe."

By Lake Baikal I had laid it all out in detail, and we had tried it, and it had failed completely.

"OK," Tom said.

I stood up and walked over to the barrow pit. The wind hit me. I got down on my hands and knees and found seven small stones and brought them back behind the haystack. I squeezed into my old spot, brushed away an empty space on the ground, and laid the stones in a line. I gouged an arrow into the soil. The arrow pointed directly into the line of stones.

Tom said, "I guess before we go Mark wants to say something."

Everyone turned toward me. They looked tired and muddled.

"I've said this before," I said.

I pointed to the arrow. "*Veter.*"

I pointed to the seven stones in a line. "*Nas.*"

Everyone nodded. I began to explain and Tanya translated.

"This is the way a team rides. It is called paceline riding. We are a team and we should do it. One for all and all for one sort of thing."

Tom and Torie grinned. They thought I was naive for trying to explain it again.

"The rider in front *pulls, drafts,* for everyone else. The front rider cleaves the wind." I put my finger on the stone at the front of the line facing into the arrow.

Fyodor and Pavel and Natasha looked bored.

"The front rider cleaves the wind and the rest pedal behind, front wheel to rear wheel. Like elephants trundling nose to tail, or ducks swimming beak to butt." This made Tanya smile.

"It is asinine for each of us to be fighting the wind on our own."

No one said a thing. I remembered a few numbers from studying the physics of bicycling in college.

"At thirty miles per hour, eighty-five percent of a rider's energy is used to cut a hole through the air with his body. Right now we're all cutting our own holes."

Everyone nodded. That was a bad sign.

"In an effective paceline, the effort expended by each rider in the chain is successively diminished until the cyclist at the back is spinning almost effortlessly, pulled along by the wedge of bicyclists before him. Solidarity."

"Mark, just explain how it works would you," Tom said.

"The lead rider drafts for say three miles, then swings out left, allows the line to slide past on his right and then drops in behind the last rider." I shuffled the front stone to the end of the line.

"The new leader pulls for three miles and then the circle shifts again." I shuffled back the second stone. "And so on."

Everyone nodded.

We got back up on the highway. The wind was slamming down the road. We rolled off and formed up and were flying together for perhaps a mile and it was wonderful and it worked and we were a wing through the wind smooth and powerful and indomitable and then the Soviets gave up. Tanya was in front plugging away and Fyodor swung around her and charged past and Pavel and Natasha took after him.

At the next haystack, after we had a long nap, I tried again. I laid out the stones and drew an arrow.

"In paceline riding it is necessary to ride together. The distance between one cyclist's rear wheel and the next cyclist's front wheel should be less than a foot. That's where the wind pocket is." I crowded my stones close together.

The Soviets looked around languidly. They knew I was talking to them. I attempted to explain a few more things, then gave up.

We tried it again. Fyodor pulled too fast, Pavel refused to hold a straight line, Natasha refused to pull at all. She rode right behind Fyodor. He was the best windbreak because he never curled over his handlebars. He rode with his back erect as a billboard. Natasha stayed right on his wheel. It was obvious she knew exactly how to ride in a paceline. She dropped back when he dropped back, avoiding her pull completely.

Tom talked to them at the next stop. He said something oblique about cowardice but they didn't catch it. The day was a failure. We all ended up riding alone against the wind.

That night, exhausted, we wobbled off the road and fell behind another haystack. Wind bit through our tents into our dreams and morning came in a blink and the earth was still brown and shaking and out of focus with straw zinging off the haystack like arrows. The fire blew itself out and the tea turned cold and the tents almost tore from our hands when we packed up.

Another day of solo thrashing, the flatness so constant it could make you believe the earth was flat.

And another day, another another another.

One night we lay down with the wind and by now we were used to it but sometime during the compacting blacking, it stopped. We woke up because our tents quit snapping. In the morning, it was autumn.

Frost lay heavy as snow in the field. Frozen fog hung over the earth. Torie and I crunched over gelid hummocks carrying water from the creek. Our noses were running and the damp chill of the earth rose up under our chins and the sun was different, not high and fierce and vain, but low and jaundiced.

"It is fall," I said. It was the middle of August.

"Naw," Torie said.

"It's fall now," I said to Tom back at the campfire. He was silently plunking potatoes into the pot of water hung over the flames. He shook his head. Torie and Tom were from Seattle.

Tanya and the Soviets knew by instinct that in Siberia fall
came in August. Just as it does in Wyoming.

That morning we put wool socks on our hands and dissolved
into the gnawing fog. Our toes froze hard and our cheeks froze
red and our eyes glistened. Moisture soaked through our socks
and our hands became as numb and unwieldy as lobster claws.
All the heat settled in our stomachs and we rode with no hands,
and no feet and no head. We rode coveting the sun until it
finally came out and burned away the bushy whiteness and the
highway turned a shiny wet black.

Just when our fingers and toes and earlobes were tingling,
the wind came back. And the road quit.

The paving machines were hardened in at the end of the last
block of pavement. Haggard men were standing around in
billowing dirtcaked overalls. Beyond the dead paving machines
a dirt road continued into the plain. It was a one-lane dirt road
that disappeared into clouds of dust.

Tom got out our map. On it the road was a mendaciously
thick red line.

We dropped into our lowest gear, dropped our heads,
dropped down onto the road and vanished into a blizzard of
dirt.

Dirt in our teeth dirt in our hair dirt so thick in our ears we
couldn't hear. Dirt in our eyes abrading our eyeballs and dirt in
the folds of our skin and dirt up our asses and penises and
vaginas.

We each rode alone.

One day we met a cowboy.

He was on a black horse in the howling. We were out of food
and out of water and had no idea how far the next village was.
The cowboy was neither asleep nor awake moving his cattle
across the road.

He leaned out of his saddle to get a good look at us. He wore
a fur cap with the flaps down and a heavy coat. His hands held
the reins and rested on the horn of the saddle and the dirt was
squalling around him and around us and I realized this was the
way it had always been. The Mongols and the Huns and a
hundred others. All nomads all living in hell without so much
as blinking pushing themselves and their cattle or sheep or

goats across the colossal plains with omniscient grace and mer-
cilessness.

"Do you know where the next village is?" yelled Tanya.

He nodded and squinched up his eyes.

"Where?"

"Go back. Go back till you see a field on your right with a
path by it. The path goes to a village."

His horse took him away into the stream of beasts.

We wheeled around. The wind picked us up and threw us so
hard down the road we almost missed the path. The path
wound through a cornfield. The stalks blew sideways and
scratched our arms and legs. Beyond the cornfield was the
village.

There was a well in the middle of the street. Small wooden
homes with shutters flopping like broken arms faced each other
across the dirt. The tin roofs screeched. Red dust clouded out
the sky as if the fields and forests surrounding the village were
on fire.

We gathered under the roof of the well, dropped the bucket
in the hole and pulled up water. The water entered us like
electricity. It shocked us it was so cold. We had been sweating
riding hard as we possibly could ride and now we were stopped
standing in the wind with freezing water inside us. We began to
shiver.

Tanya ran across the dirt squeezing her shoulders. She
knocked on the doors of the huts in the storm. They looked
abandoned but they weren't. They were preparing for winter.
She brought back bread and milk.

We ate under the roof of the well with our backs against the
tempest. Just as we were about to set out again, a military truck
came out of the pouring dirt. It gimped up to the well and died.

Three men dropped out of the cab. They wore green wool
uniforms with high shabby black boots. Their uniforms were
dusty and their necks chafed and they were laughing and joking and smiling. They were young. They slapped us on the back
and shook our hands.

They didn't notice the frigid wind. They splashed each other
with the ice water and dirt streaks ran down their necks. They
were not cold or thin. They looked strong and robust.

One was an officer. He had seen us on TV. He insisted we

autograph his passport. Then the other two insisted we sign their passports, right beside their black-and-white photos. The ink smeared our names and globs of flying dirt caught in it like flies in honey but they banged their passports shut and shoved them back in their breast pockets and brought out the vodka.

"We celebrate your great adventure!" the officer said.

They passed around the bottle of vodka and said don't worry we have more and of course they did because they were young and making away with as much as they could before they had to go back to their own dirt village. They said don't worry we have more but that's not why we didn't want any. We were weak. The well water alone had been like vodka.

Then the officer shouted, "I have a present for you!"

He was elated because an idea had come to him. He ran into the gale around to the back of his truck. He came back with the present.

"*Dlya vas. Ot nas.*" For you. From us.

He handed it ceremoniously to Fyodor.

"We hit it with the truck. It was flying all by itself."

It was road kill. Its head was crushed flat and bloody with dirt caked in the blood and bones and brains spilling out, but the body was perfect. Smooth and elegant and strong and you would have thought it was alive if you hadn't seen the head.

Fyodor got out his ax. He took the goose by the neck, whacked off the head, whacked off the wings and then skinned it. We had goose for dinner over the campfire.

35

FROST CLOAKED THE earth in the morning. We dumped the pot, picked the leftover pieces of goose out of the grass, and rode off into the wind.

Tom, Torie, Tanya and I let the Soviets go ahead of us, then we began working together. We got in a tight line and rode in concert. We circled and the next person pulled and then we circled again. We did it and did it. By noon we were pacelining fluidly. We winged past the Soviets. They hopped on our tail. We were two separate teams now, for good.

At lunch we stopped in another village. We had no food so I stood in a long line that went out into the dirt. The others went in search of water.

I was the only man in a line of big women. Some were old and crippled and had walked here from their cabins. The others had come from the factory, standing packed in the back of a flatbed with their eyes closed and their hands over their mouths because of the dust. This was the only time you could come if you wanted to get something. They were all square peasant women. We were standing in line together and they were talking to each other the way women do when they are by themselves and I felt strange because I was not a woman. Women stood in line for food. Men stood in line for vodka. This was understood so the women were looking at me hard over the edge of their round cheeks. After a while they began turning their great bodies and looking at me straight on and smiling uninhibitedly so I began to feel all right. They knew I was a foreigner. They had seen me come to their village on a bicycle. They tried talking to me and it didn't work too well but it didn't matter. I was one of them, accepted not as a man, for that would be intolerable, but as a foreigner who needed food. Eventually we got through the door. Inside was a small dark room with a wood desk in the center. There was a large crate on the desk and a woman, a clerk, standing behind it. There was a painting of Him behind her. The women did not talk and laugh as much inside. The broad back of the woman in front of me touched me and the broad chest of the woman in back of me touched me. We were all taking small steps, moving together. When it was my turn and I was in front of the desk, I handed my money to the clerk and asked for four loaves. She shook her head. It was too many. She was about to yell at me when the woman who had been in front of me came back and took one of hers out of her string bag and put it back into the crate. The clerk returned to her a few raggy bills. Then the woman behind me began telling the clerk something and I understood some of it. The clerk smiled at me. She shoved the money I had given her into her apron pocket and made me hold out my arms in a cradle. Then she carefully stacked four large loaves against my chest.

I came out and the others were waiting. They had found water. We ate the bread and drank the water and then pedaled. We pedaled the wind and chewed the dirt and drank the bread and ate the water and pedaled and pedaled until one evening.

We stopped in the gleaming green field of a cathedral. The cathedral rose above the village like a dream. Big as a dream. Big as a big pink storm cloud grown right from the soil of the village. It rose so far in the sky we had been seeing it for miles. Miles and miles we aimed for it and ground into the wind not looking up because it didn't seem to get closer. We ground and ground and finally wound between the log houses to the cathedral. Then the wind quit as if we had bicycled right through the arched doors and on inside and stopped on the kneeworn stones feeling so tiny, the vaulted ceilings going up higher than even the sky and the light coming through the stained panes like starlight. Even from the outside you could feel most of that because the walls of the cathedral were still standing even with all the black holes in them.

There was a woman in the field also staring at the cathedral. We stopped beside her. We were all standing staring because the light was that kind of light that never happens in cities or even towns. The magic light that comes only to small villages where there is such a cathedral to glow upon. It makes you believe you believe in something even if you don't or don't know what it is. The old woman turned to us and said she could still see the tanks coming up the dirt road and surrounding the church. She had her gray head in a black wool scarf and wore black wool stockings and black shoes as if it had happened this morning. She said all the people from the village had gathered inside the cathedral and locked arms and were singing and the soldiers had dragged them out. She said she began to cry and her children asked her why she was crying. The tanks surrounded the church and the light was just like this she said. Gleaming. She said one of the village children screamed and escaped and ran to the cathedral just when the commander shoved away all the women and dropped his arm and the men in the tanks leaned quietly back in the cradle of their seats inside their tanks, and fired. And the wail of the women silenced the sound of the guns. The guns made no sound the old woman said. Then she took a loaf of bread from her basket and gave it to us.

We ate the bread and pedaled the wind and drank the dirt and pedaled and pedaled until one evening.

We found a workers' hotel in a village. In the lobby there was one table with two metal buckets on top. A woman came out of a door and asked us what we wanted. She had a black eye. Her lower lip was cut so she talked shyly with one hand in front of her mouth. We said we wanted rooms for the night. She said there were no rooms available. Behind her was a man smoking, his belly squashed against the doorknob. We had been riding for days in dirt. Our teeth were glutinous with dirt and our throats bloated with dirt. Dirt running in our blood like salt. We wanted rooms. Please, the woman said. Tanya looked at the man in the doorway and said she would find a phone and call the police. The woman unconsciously touched the skin above

her eye. She took Tanya aside while we waited in the lobby. We
were thirsty. We pushed away the dead flies on top of the water
in the buckets.

When we were registered the woman led us down a corridor
and unlocked four doors. They were splintered like doors in a
vandalized building.

Torie and I shared a small room with no light bulb. It had
walls that bowed in and a floor that bulged up. There were two
metal beds. No mattresses. The sheets had not been cleaned
since the last visitors. There was a pillow with yellow stains. We
sat down on the beds and the springs screeched and cockroaches ran out between our feet.

The bathroom, Torie said smiling.

She wanted me to have a look. She thought it was funny and
laughed which made me laugh too. The bathroom was in a
corner of the room. I opened the door and stench spumed out
of the dark. I shut the door. Torie found a candle and lit it. I
opened the door again, stepped one foot in and set the candle
on the sink.

Don't think you want to come in here, I said.

The toilet was smeared green and brown and piled with human feces. It had flooded over many times so visitors were
shitting on top of the lid. There were piles of shit in the bathtub
and fingerprints on the walls.

There was a rusty stream of water coming from one of the
spigots on the sink. I washed the dirt out of my mouth and ears
and nose. Then I felt something on my legs and leapt and
stomped and heard crunching and looked down. The floor was
black and trembling, the cockroaches so thick they were on top
of each other. I stepped out and closed the bathroom door
behind me.

Quite an experience, I said grinning.

That's what I thought, said Torie.

The hotel had no restaurant. The woman had said there was
a bar beneath the hotel. We'd all agreed to meet in the bar after
cleaning up. Torie squirted water from her waterbottle on a
handkerchief and wiped the dirt off her fingers one by one.
Then she wiped her face and neck and said, ready or not, and
we left.

To get to the bar we had to go around the back of the hotel

through the garbage. Behind the hotel was an entrance that came up out of the ground. There was loud music coming out of the hole. We descended, our feet feeling for the steps. At the bottom it smelled like alcohol and vomit. Everyone else was already there.

It was a disco. Deafening music and black vinyl chairs and black tables and black walls with shards of mirror glued on like pieces from a car accident. There was a small cement dance floor. The ceiling was low with pipes hanging down like intestines. It was too loud to talk.

We had some indistinguishable food and then ordered champagne. It was the only alcohol they had. The barmaid carried the bottles over through the gushy underground air. She was a young plump tired woman but she smiled. She was the only person working in the bar.

There were a few men at other tables. They were drinking and spilling their drinks and hitting each other and shouting at the barmaid and drinking and slumping over. They had rubbery black faces. They clomped in and sat down and got up and staggered out and were replaced by other men like them.

At a table beside us were two men and a young woman. The men were shouting and strutting. The young woman was laughing at the right times. They were friends of the barmaid. She brought them bottles of champagne and took away the empty ones before the men broke them.

Once the barmaid sat down for a moment beside the young woman, carefully holding the empty bottles in her lap. They talked and laughed. They laughed the laugh that was silent and different from the one they used for men. I saw the young woman slip something in the barmaid's apron pocket. The barmaid put her hand over it. Then the woman must have felt something because her eyes came up and looked at me and then let go as if throwing a bad fish back into the water.

I drank a bottle of warm champagne and the Soviets left to go to bed. Somehow one of the men at the table next to us found out we were Americans. He was the young woman's boyfriend. He came over to our table and stood right above me and rammed his finger into my chest several times and yelled *AMIRIKANSKI! AMIRIKANSKI!* Tanya stood up and he looked at her breasts and forgot about me for a minute and reached out and she stepped back and snapped at him and his eyes flashed and he remembered I was still sitting there so he bent over me and cocked his arm in front of my face and flexed. He clenched his fist and rocked his arm back and forth flexing screaming *AMIRIKANSKI! AMIRIKANSKI!* down on the top of my head. I looked up and smiled at him in the face. He screamed louder. I turned my head and smiled at Tanya. She flinched. She stood up and pulled the boyfriend onto the dance floor and danced one song and then got him seated back at his table. I said, Thank you Tanya. She didn't look at me.

It was hard for me not to look at the young woman. She had short blond hair pulled back. She wore a loose gray V-neck sweater and a pleated, old-fashioned green skirt that came to her knees and her legs were long as a deer's. She was here with these two men, but she wasn't. She was laughing when they tried to make her laugh but she wasn't.

It got late and the bar closed. The blackrubber men at the other tables disappeared. Tom let his eyes close for just a moment and then slept sitting up with half a glass of champagne in his hand before he woke with a jerk and left. Then there was just that young woman, and her friend the barmaid, and the two men and Tanya and Torie and me and the dark and the earsplitting music.

The same manboy saw me again and stood up and kicked his chair over backward and screamed *AMIRIKANSKI!* and started toward me but stumbled on the fallen chair. I rose slowly feeling my hands close feeling the muscles in my back hoping with all my heart he would make it back to his feet but the barmaid was already there. She put a bottle of champagne in his hands and he sat down. The young woman looked at me while I was standing there and I thought she would smile but her expression was blank. I sat down.

The barmaid went back behind the bar and shut off the music. Noiselessness fell over us like a coat. I turned in my seat to look at the barmaid. She took the tape from her apron and put it in the player.

It started very slow and quiet. Simple notes. A song. A song good as silence. A sad Russian folk song. It rounded the edges off the pieces of glass on the walls and washed the vinyl chairs and filled in the chips on the tables. It came slowly and cleaned the cobwebs off the ceiling and pushed the herniated pipes back up inside the hotel.

I looked at Torie. Her eyes were wet. Tanya was swaying.

I looked at the young woman. She was already standing. The two men were bent forward, their heads dangling on their chests like birds with broken necks. The woman stepped away from the table onto the dance floor and began to twirl. She twirled slowly, the music rising and diving and rising again and she would rise too with her skirt going out fluttering and her head gone back and then the music would fall and she would just keep turning and floating knowing the music would rise again. Her boyfriend struggled to his feet and reached out for her but he could not touch her. She knew she would carry him home. She knew she would carry him forever and she would not dance with him now. The barmaid again was there and set him back in his chair. Then the barmaid began to dance. They danced together. They danced the dance of woeman, not man. Man all manboys with cocks and balls shoving pushing fucking fighting fucking fighting to die in a bottle or battle. Not woeman. Not woeman dancing so light their feet could not touch the ground knowing already what men never know and dancing anyway. Swaying and twirling and circling together until the sound slowly disappeared. There was a song but no sound. Just the two of them holding hands dancing, and dancing, and dancing.

36

WE ESCAPED BACK into the prairie before dawn. The four of us clumped together and the Soviets bicycled on their own but none of us could go very fast or very hard. We couldn't understand why until it finally dawned on us that we were not just weak, we were weakening.

After months of water from wells just a garden away from the outhouse, and food from greasy *stalovayas* without running water, and wind indivisible as God, and dirt, we'd been worn down. We would not be strong again until we slept for a month and we would not sleep for a month until we were done.

Done?

We were close enough now that it was safe to start thinking about it. In spite of the wind, we were making eighty miles a day. Beyond this ocean of dirt were the Ural Mountains, beyond the Urals, Moscow, then down a black brick road to Leningrad. If we didn't look between our legs at the seconds sliding so slow through the dirt and blacked out the minutes and forgot the hours and forgave the days and bundled everything into weeks, the Baltic no longer seemed so far away.

"Less than a month maybe," said Tanya. We were lying on our backs in a barrow pit in the swirling dirt.

"Six weeks?" said Torie.

"*Dva myesyatsya,*" said Natasha. Two months.

"*Nyet!*" said Tanya.

"It depends on the road," I said.

Fyodor growled.

"What did he say?"

"He said, 'Depends on the snow,' " said Tanya.

"After all the shit and mud and wind?" Tom was incredulous. He snatched up a handful of dirt and flung it in the wind. "Snow would be a fucking joy!"

Sometimes when you're talking big the world will come quickly up behind you and sucker punch you in the kidneys and leave you there on the ground gasping. But then sometimes when you're talking big but truly believe, and know what you're up against, and your blood is still hot even if your bones are tired, the world can take a shine to you. Just for your hubris.

When we stood up the wind had swung about and we had a roaring tailwind.

We got on our bikes and brown fields began chuttering by like frames in an old cowboy movie. Miles and minutes and hours blew beneath us. We flew flat out and dared not stop. We needed to rest but dared not stop needed to piss but dared not stop needed to eat but dared not stop. Stopping would have been blasphemous. Like stopping in sex to get a sandwich. Nothing is more sinful than squandering a tailwind.

When night came we had taken 119 miles. We stood with our panting bikes on the steps of a hotel looking over the smoggy Irtysh River. We were in Omsk, the largest city on the West Siberian Plain.

Later that evening the rumplesuits found us drunk and dancing willynilly in the hotel restaurant. They informed us that because we were the first Americans to visit Omsk, a special tour had been arranged for the following day.

"NO!" cried Tom from the dance floor.

"No thank you," I said.

We had two days of rest planned in Omsk and we planned to rest. The rumplesuits were visibly outraged.

"Sleep," I said, and bent my head onto my hand.

In the morning, a lightning-bright boxheaded morning, they beat on our rooms until we paraded out and boarded their damn tour bus.

"Welcome, ladies and gentlemen, the first monument we will see is eighteen and one half meters high."

That's the first thing she said to us. The bus caromed across traffic and we were hungover and almost puked and she stood sturdy in the aisle—paradigm of the Soviet tour guide: sexless, voice from another planet, schoolmarmish with blazing nightmarish makeup. Several rumplesuits in dark sunglasses sat at the back of the bus. It was a two-hour tour all over Omsk and they never moved their heads or spoke a word. I thought they might be fake, like those test dummies they use in car crashes.

The first monument was a monument to the dead. The figures were bold and blocky and subtleless. If they'd been red, they could have sprung from any of the tenement placards we'd passed.

"This monument is seven and one quarter meters high," she said describing the second monument which like all monuments all over the world was a monument to the dead who died unnecessarily.

"Ladies and gentlemen, this monument is sixteen meters high," Tom said in my ear while we stood at the base of the third monument.

"Ladies and gentlemen, this monument is sixteen and one half meters high."

Then we raced across town with our police escort, one yellow car in front and one in back sirens wailing blue lights whirring. They stopped traffic at every intersection so we could reach in minutes the museum of the prison where Fyodor Dostoyevsky spent four years.

We walked through dark halls staring at fuzzy photographs. Dirt and wire and mud and emaciated men with hollow eyes.

I asked the guide if she thought there were any Dostoyevskys presently out there anywhere in Siberia and she looked at me and I saw something in her eyes and in the muscles of her jaw but thought she really didn't understand the question.

We visited one final monument for the hundreds of thousands who died in a war no one outside the Soviet Union would ever have known about, then were taken to a banquet.

It was held in a huge hall inside what was once a cathedral. Our tour guide was apparently not invited. She was ducking out the door when I touched her arm.

"Excuse me. Could you please tell me why almost all Communist party administrations are headquartered in ex-churches?"

Everyone else had passed in. We were alone in the doorway.

"You are a smart one aren't you," she said with a voice suddenly different, suddenly soft. She studied me for a moment. She was carefully wiping off the makeup around one eye with a tissue.

"You've been here for a while I know, and you've been lucky and seen what no one else has ever seen. But you are still only traveling. *Just* traveling. Don't think you know everything." Her voice was intelligent and feminine. She folded over the tissue and began cleaning her other eye.

"I would have thought you knew that one by now."

I didn't know what she was talking about. Her voice and her eyes and the new strange tremoring of her body had shaken me. I'd completely forgotten what I had asked her.

"Obviously because communism is a religion, not a government. You think you have been thinking, but you have not." She wiped off her red lipstick.

"And because the buildings are better and more elegant, better for our clergy, our bureaucrats, you know." She turned to go.

The heavily scrolled door was slamming when she slipped her fingers back in, just at the moment when the weight of the door would have broken her hand, and caught it, gracefully. I was still standing there, struck dumb. She looked through the crack.

"Yes," she said, "I think so."

I wrinkled my face. She shook her head despairingly.

"To your question in the museum."

37

THE BANQUET TABLES were covered with white linen. There were bouquets placed every five feet and Pepsi and chocolates and candies and rumplesuits and their wives and folks from something called the People's Peace Committee and the clergy, two Russian Orthodox priests, and a handful of Omsk personalities, and us. We were the guests of honor.

A portly woman from the People's Peace Committee stood at a podium and began a lengthy speech in seamless Soviet. She said her speech was about the people of Omsk. She listed the # of factories and the # of workers and the # of widgets made in every factory and the # of rubles being spent on this or that and the # of . . . and somehow I stopped her in mid-spit-and-polish to ask if it might not be more important to just decently feed all the people and she didn't miss a beat and said there was more than enough food that food was plentiful everywhere and available to everyone and where did I get such an absurd idea and went on with her speech. After a while she sat down and everyone clapped.

Then the older priest with a gray beard down to his plate now covered with candy wrappers stood up. He said he would not give us numbers as she had and chuckled and went on to tell us the # of churches being restored and the # of parishioners and the # of young people returning to the church and the # of wonderful happinesses he felt in his heart. When he sat down the priest beside him stood up and passed out record albums of Russian choral music and their business cards.

Then came the entertainment. A group of women in fluorescent traditional dresses bounced out hooking elbows and singing shrilly. They were singing so loudly you thought they might be trying to throw their lungs right up out of their throats. It made you look at their mouths and how wide they opened. But if you looked at their eyes, their eyes weren't singing. When it was over the portly woman asked if we had enjoyed it and everyone in the hall was looking at us as if we were little kings and queens and we said very much. She hesitated. Then she asked if we would like to hear any more music and we said of course meaning it sincerely for the most part.

She was beginning to explain when four gentlemen cut her off by romping out a side door and across the hall to our table. They were dressed in jeans. One man stepped out in front.

"Goo' dafternoon ta ye," he said. He spoke with a distinct Liverpool accent. "We're *Western Siberia*." He was talking to us. He knew no one else in the hall could understand him. He introduced the band slowly with an intentional lilt, pointing to each man.

"Sergei on that banjo. Sasha withiz guitar. Another Sergei withiz mighty guitar and even mightier harmonica. And I'm Andrew.

"They cull this one 'Bye Bye Love' but me an the group like to cull it 'If you were the last lassie on earth you culd name your price.' " He nodded, winked at us, couldn't keep himself from grinning, and turned to his friends.

One at a time they began to hum, each falling in at a different pitch. Then the guitars and the banjo started and they were off, singing with abandon, picking their instruments and thumping their feet and tossing out their song like boys singing around a campfire. They ended on a fine high note, all together, looking at each other.

We clapped and whooped and everyone else at the banquet sat still as sardines with eyes just as blank and mouths just as shut.

The men paused only for a moment, then they sang a folk

song, and then a spiritual and by then we were singing along so the portly woman tried to stop it, bending up awkwardly and spilling candy wrappers off the banquet table.

"Well I spose that's it now," Andrew said, "but we'd like to do one last one for ye. You know it I know ye do. It's called 'I Saw the Light.' "

He leaned his head back and his tenor voice soared so high you thought he'd have to lift up on his tiptoes, and he did, and his voice kept on rising and they all came in singing with their instruments and the song came to us and we hadn't heard anyone sing a song just because they loved to sing since we'd entered the country a century ago.

He lay at the back of the cabin and sang to himself. He knew already singing would help his hunger go away so he sang to himself making up the words as he went. He could hear the guitar by the fire through the dark. He kept his eyes closed so he could see the fingers flickering on the strings. His ears were his whole body, as they can be for a young boy. He could hear his uncles singing, harmonizing, the light voice and the low one. He lay still on the planks and sang softly and his voice was high and sweet and disappearing until he could not hear it only feel it inside, and then he was asleep.

In the morning, when there was still ice in the mud and mud in the sky and still no food, they left. All three on the giant horse.

They passed out of the village. The morning came in their mouths and noses like the smell of snow before it falls. They did not speak. Sound was the sound of hooves heavy as anvils thunking the frozen earth. Leaves hard as fossils in the mud.

They rode to the cemetery. The boy slid down and ran through the frostbitten grass around the rusted crosses and stone stumps. He quit running suddenly, almost falling forward. He stood still and looked down and did not know what he felt. His eyes went across the names cut in the gray stone. He could not read but it did not matter. Then he ran back. His uncles pulled him up in front and he took the reins and they rode away from the village forever.

*   *   *

When they'd finished that last song, letting it float by itself right to the top of the hall, they began to walk out. We leapt to our feet and yelled.

All four turned in unison and came back to our table. They were sweating and flushed from letting their personal happiness show in public. The woman at the podium shouted at them and we quickly agreed to meet outside the hall as soon as the banquet was over.

They rode north through the fields. They camped in the forests. They built fires and sometimes when they weren't too tired, they sang.

They skirted the cities—even less to eat there. They stayed on the curled paths in the country. Farm to farm. Sometimes they fell asleep up on their giant gray draft horse and he would keep moving.

They passed into Belorussia where they could still understand most things. They crossed into Lithuania where even the uncles could not make out the words. But work is all one language. They had the biggest horse anyone had ever seen and they worked hard so they always ate.

One day when it was whip wet and cold though none of them could notice now because they were used to living outside, they rode into Königsberg.

Another speech began. The obligatory speech about our bravery and how we would live for the rest of our lives knowing we were the first people on earth to bicycle from one end of the Soviet Union to the other.

Then the woman at the podium said that since we were sportsmen we would enjoy the next item on the agenda, a sports colosseum, where we would learn the # of seats it held and the # of games and # of . . .

We agreed to go just so the banquet would end. We were veterans at this. *Western Siberia* was waiting for us when we got out in the hall. We reversed ourselves immediately and refused to go and the People's Peace Committee was mortified. The Soviets went with the Soviets and we invited the band up to my hotel room.

*   *   *

They had planned all along to take him. But a man with a limp told them they must not. He sold fruit on the wharf and gave them three apples for nothing.

"Your great horse could end up in the kettle if the weather is unkind and the journey long. And it will be."

So the afternoon before they were to sail, the boy rode him back. He rode back two days' journey in one to a farmer. It was dusk and the farmer was still working hard in his field. Their horse had pulled stones from the man's field for three days. The man had asked if he could guide the horse and he could and he had been gentle.

The boy had already spoken gravely to his horse during the ride back. He said good-bye and when his feet touched the ground, he ran.

The three steamed together to Argentina in the bowels of an old ship and all three lived and not everyone did. And the boy dreamed about his giant horse and how he was alive and heaving stones from the earth of his home and he cried and sang to himself in the dark.

When they landed they walked down the plank together into the yellow dirt and horrible heat and a sweating fat man sniggered "can you ride that horse" and Fyodor Mazihevich didn't understand one word and walked over and climbed up easily and the horse didn't move a muscle. So Fyodor and his uncles became cowboys, gauchos.

They learned to take the heat as well as the cold. They learned another language. They nearly died from unknown diseases and bites from unknown bugs. They built campfires on the high plains under stars that were not the same stars and when they weren't too tired, they sang.

Being ordinary Soviets, they were forbidden to enter our hotel at night. But we snuck them in and rushed the floor lady and got past her, all cramming into my room and slamming the door. They got out their instruments and gathered on the bed.

"Ye know, there iz nothing on this earth as special as playing for people who understand why," Andrew said.

He couldn't look us in the eye after saying this so he just bent down over his guitar and began to play.

*   *   *

All three always worked together. They lived outside. They lived with horses and cattle and dust and snow and moved all around a country they somehow could not learn to love because another geography was already inside them. They were gauchos until their homesickness finally burst over them one night singing a Russian ballad. They shot out on the three good horses and stole others from people who had cheated them and galloped day after night all the way back to the dock with the yellow dirt and the heat they could not notice now.

Ships had changed and they couldn't all sail back to Russia together. The uncles went first. Fyodor, who could speak four languages and ride any horse on earth but could still not read or write, left a week later. By the time his ship reached Canada he had let his hatred pass through him and he still believed he would soon be back home with his uncles.

But distance builds up a new life and Quebec needed no cowboys and it was only because he spoke Spanish that he got work as a sailor.

He sailed around the world. Many times. He grew to know the man Magellan must have been by the Strait itself. He understood Cortés and Columbus. He learned all this and had his adventure and when the cargo was good he sent donations to the Soviet Red Cross.

Then one afternoon in Liverpool he married a freckled, fair-haired young woman named Matilda. He had fallen in love with her laugh because it was young and light and he had done well what young men must do and had become old ahead of his years in all the doing and a light laugh was worth giving up all the fog over the rolling blue sea for fog on the rolling green hills.

The loneliest songs ever written *Western Siberia* sang for us. They sang of a geography they had never seen that was already inside them.

We'd bought as many bottles of champagne and beer and vodka as we could. The boys could drink. And they played better when they drank. Sweeter. Propped up against the wall singing with their eyes closed and their tongues smooth and their fingers moving on their own.

*   *   *

They were happy because they were happy. They had two good sons, Andrei and Kizov. They were given Russian names because in all this time Fyodor had not forgotten Russia. Not a day of it. He sent letters to his old village even though they were never answered. He sent donations to the Red Army during the Great Patriotic War. He could remember riding his giant horse while his father walked in the field. He could remember the mud between the squat log cabins. He could remember the sky was bigger and soil darker and snow deeper and rain cleaner as all old men remember the geography of their childhood.

So one morning he had to go. Matilda disagreed. So did his first son, Andrei. "You are English," Fyodor said, "I am Russian." Andrei had a pregnant wife and a passable job and refused to go. But Kizov was a young man. He would go and visit and when he had had enough he would leave and travel around the world like his father and when he was ready he would find a beautiful wife in a faraway port and have his own two sons.

So old man Fyodor and his youngest son, Kizov, packed their leather suitcases and donned the gray wool suits they wore only to church and came down the stairs to find Matilda in the doorway wearing the flowered dress she had worn when she'd laughed for Fyodor without even knowing his last name. She was wearing a bonnet, her trim suitcase on the floor beside her.

They took a ship because Fyodor insisted. Fyodor thought he was returning to Russia. He sang songs out on the deck for Matilda. His eyes watered. He told a hundred stories true only to him.

"You are born with a stone from your home deep inside you," he said. "That stone is magnetic. And when the time comes, that land will pull you back."

They sang and we sang with them. The sound of the music went inside us. The guitars and the banjo and the harmonica.

The floor lady came once and whopped on our door and we did not open it and expected the rumplesuits with the police to show up because singing softly with friends in a hotel room in the city of Omsk is illegal. But they never came. Then the lights went off in our room and we knew they'd been shut off and I heard Andrew laugh, and we kept right on singing.

*   *   *

When they arrived it was 1960. They were questioned by the customs officials over and over. Why had they come to the Soviet Union? Why had they come to the Soviet Union?

Matilda was frightened. Kizov was silent. Fyodor was proud. He spoke in Russian and told them exactly why. He told them what he had told Matilda on the boat. But they did not speak Russian. Eventually he became angry and shouted.

"Look at the passports, look at the visas."

They said, "What passports? What visas?"

It was just before dawn and our eyes were the only light spots left in the room.

"B'forr we go," said Andrew, "I'd like t'sing ye a ballad I wrote. It's about me family."

They were never allowed to leave. Fyodor Mazihevich, and his wife, Matilda, and his son Kizov, were settled by the government in Western Siberia, in a village three thousand miles from where Fyodor had lived as a boy.

Kizov spoke no Russian. He was a dreamy English boy. Fyodor was forced to go back to work and when he became too old Kizov began to work for him. Kizov was bright. He had learned the language well by then. He had learned the system and let most of the hatred pass through him. Back then he still thought he was going to get out. He worked in the fields and in the factories and did things on the side to put away money and the years passed.

He sang often to himself because he knew it would help. He sang the English songs his father had sung to him and the old Russian songs his father had sung to him and one day at the market he met a woman who heard his voice. She looked like his mother he thought. She would laugh when no one else would. She taught him in secret the Russian folk songs you could never sing in the market. He fell in love and married her.

And they were happy because they were happy. They had two children. They sang to them as they were growing up. One was named Olga, the other, Andrew.

38

We left Omsk on asphalt. We wouldn't let ourselves think about it.

A rumplesuit at the banquet had said it was all asphalt after Omsk. All the way to Leningrad. He'd said it in the same voice that the woman at the banquet had said there was food for everyone. We still had our own faith in the emasculatability of all things.

We rode out of Omsk as two separate teams. The four of us pacelined, tight and fast and together. The asphalt was so smooth you didn't have to think about riding. I thought about all the banquets we had attended. I thought about the one in Krasnoyarsk.

I had complimented a rumplesuit on the superb Soviet highways. I'd laid it on thick. The rumplesuit had bobbled his jowls and said sincerely, Of course there is pavement, how absurd, what kind of a country do you think this is? Sasha was sitting next to me. I asked him, Who are these people in the Communist party? He wouldn't answer. Sasha, I said, what does it take to become one of these people? He smiled forlornly. We were at a table with a crowd of them. He turned sideways and I turned sideways and he spoke quietly in his Russian British.

"Well, let me say first, they are paid ten times what we are

237

paid. They have good homes. They have good food and clothes from the West."

"So you're smart, you could use a new suit, why not play the game?"

Sasha flinched. "It is *not* a game, Mark. Never forget this. You have come here and you will get to leave and go home and write your stories. They will always be stories for you. *I* must stay here. I must live here."

His face went calm again. "Well you see. They will get a car when they are young so they will not have to take the buses. They will have many friends. They will all have the same friends. They will get beer and meat and soap when there is no beer and no meat and no soap anywhere."

"But . . ." He cut me off.

"Their babushka will not have to work until she dies in her garden. Their children will go to elite schools. Their wives and their daughters will wear French makeup." He stopped. He was waiting for me to speak but I didn't.

"Very well then. Now. There are three ways to become part of this party." It was a pun. Sasha had intended it.

"You must get girls, get money, or *zdyelat' atsos*."

I looked at him.

"You are naive." He rested his elbows on his knees and let his head sink into his palms.

"You have to do these things to get in. Then you have to do them and things like them for the rest of your life."

I still did not understand. I shook my head.

"Girls," he began. "Little girls, big girls, little boys, young boys. Girls. Whores and prostitutes. Bring them to your local party official.

"Number two, money. Not rubles. American dollars or German marks. You do what you must do, however you must do it, and give this money to your party official for what you want and he will be impressed and believe you are someone. Maybe you can be put into an election. Sometimes, now days, people my age are born into families with money. Sometimes people still remember what their parents did to get this money.

"And number three, *zdyelat' atsos*." He looked at me and smiled and then frowned. "I am sorry, I do not know the translation for this."

Sasha took a pen from his suit and bent studiously over the banquet table. He drew a small picture on his napkin.

"I am sorry," he said, "this is a bad drawing, but, well you see, it means more." I looked at the drawing.

"Blowjob."

"*Atsos?* Blowjob?" Sasha repeated the word and began to laugh quietly.

"Blowjob. Mark, I like your language. I do. Blowjob. That is a very nice metaphor."

But now it *was* asphalt, strip after strip laid end to end and melted together like long pieces of black licorice.

The wind was still against us because the world was still turning the same direction but it didn't feel like it. It felt as if the whole world had changed—the way it feels when you've had winter for months and one day you wake up and the sun's already out and warm and you get that tickly feeling in your chest as if something remarkable and good is going to happen. We had been in a sea of gray dirt for three thousand miles.

We rode ninety-two miles, ninety-seven miles, ninety-nine miles, ninety-three miles, without a thought. It was autumn in Siberia and rained constant cold rain that hardened our fingers so when we wiped the snot off our faces it felt as if we were wiping with a hunk of wood, but we still made the miles.

One day when it was so cold it was sleeting, we had to stop. We went to a village market and bought handwoven wool hats and mittens and socks. Babushkas made them and sold them to us cackling about how warm they would be and how gaunt and frozen we looked.

We began to build fires at lunch. We huddled around the damp flames and drank hot water until our feet and fingers came back and we could ride again. In the villages, we went inside *stalovayas* even when we couldn't stand the smell just to escape the rain.

We reached Chelyabinsk on September 24. We had crossed the West Siberian Plain. We were still on asphalt. It was pouring rain.

Our hotel did not have heat, so we went to dinner in a fancy restaurant that did. Just the four of us, the Soviets went to bed.

Tanya bribed the maître d' to let us in then bribed the waiter to get us served and once more to get extra champagne. The band played the same song seven times in a row and the decor was androgynous mythical workers marching across the wall-paper but the food was quite good and the champagne continuous and we got limber and danced.

Sometime in the evening a gentleman from the table next to ours began talking to Tanya. His name was Sergei. We were invited to his table for a drink. A toast.

There were four of them, two men and two women, and four of us, and we were well into riotous talking and toasting when the restaurant closed. It was ten-thirty. All eight of us packed into Sergei's car and shot through the wet dark city to a two-room apartment.

The apartment belonged to a friend of theirs named Sasha. He and his wife and their child, Serosha, were sleeping. When we arrived they hastily folded up the couch. Serosha had fallen asleep on a blanket on the floor with a Matrioshka doll all taken apart, the different heads and bodies mixed up. They lifted him carefully, blanket and all, and put him back to sleep in the kitchen. They set up two card tables and brought out their best wine and cheese.

When we first rode into Chelyabinsk, Tom and I had searched all over town for cheese. In every shop we were told there was no cheese in Chelyabinsk. I asked Tanya to ask Sasha how he came to have wine and cheese.

"Of course there is cheese," said Sasha. "They have cheese." He spread out his large hands. His chest was a foot and a half thick. He had been a world-class kayaker. He was talking about the rumplesuits.

"How did you get cheese?" I asked.

"There is plenty of food in our country," Sasha said and laughed. I couldn't tell if he was joking or not.

I thought perhaps Sasha and Sergei were rumplesuits in disguise but Tanya pealed with giggles and said I was a poor judge of character and we toasted this or that again and I forgot my question.

Tanya talked and talked and Tom and Torie and I drank and laughed and understood less and less but it was an abso-

lutely splendid evening. I do not remember how we got back to
the hotel.

A day later, when we were leaving the city bound for the
Urals, Sergei and Sasha and all the others were there to say
good-bye.

The morning was raw and raining and I was sober and rode
alone. Brilliant orange birch hung over the road and small
bright leaves drifted down onto the wet pavement. After a while
I remembered something and dropped back to ride with Tanya.

"Sasha never told me how he got the cheese," I said.

"Did you understand what we were talking about?" Tanya
said.

"Some," I said.

"You know, you must to listen closely to the words. Some
words have more than one meaning."

"I was trying."

"You weren't."

"I was drinking."

"You were having a great time."

"I was."

"Sasha is a gym teacher," Tanya said. We were splattering
side by side, trailing two arched whips of gray water, both bundled in wool.

"But no one is what they are here," Tanya said winking.

"Applies to you too then?"

"Yes."

"Sasha's friend Sergei, the handsome one, the one who invited us over to his table in the first place . . ." She hesitated. She
smiled.

"Yes."

"He has a business. You understand there are two economies
in this country. You have seen it. Everyone has a job with the
government. They are workers. They are waitresses or farmers, whatever. This is their government job and they do not
work at it, they go through it. Then everyone has their other
job. They do this at night or weekends. Usually both. This other
job is their honest work. The work they care about. They do
this work for themselves and their families."

I nodded. I did know this.

"Sasha is a gym teacher. But gym teachers make one hundred-twenty rubles a month. Not enough for cheese. So Sasha works for Sergei when he can."

She was breathing hard and we were splashing and I thought she might wreck into me but she wanted to finish.

"Sergei used to run this business and now he runs it again." She was playing with me.

"What happened?"

"He was sent to prison. He and four of his friends. They were sent to prison for starting this business."

"A bad business."

"Yes, yes," she laughed. "Noooo. They were put in prison because they *started a business*. Their own business. It was illegal to start your own business. They spent five years in prison. They were let out two years ago and started up the same business again."

The rain had stopped and the pavement was as beautiful as black glass. We were in the foothills of the Urals.

"Do you remember the Russian songs that Andrew sang? The kind of rough, hoppy ones."

"I do."

"They were prison songs. Our prisons have murderers and rapists. But many of our people in prisons, up until the last few years, were not like that."

"What were they like?"

"They were capitalists."

"You mean entrepreneurs."

"I do not know that word. They were called capitalists. They were people who tried to make money for themselves."

"Sergei was one of them?" I asked.

"Yes."

"What kind of business does he have?"

"Mark," she laughed gaily, "you will like this. He has an asphalt paving company."

39

Up the Urals. Away from the hurtful flat forever, rising through orange tunnels as if gravity itself were letting us go.

The beauty of land swelling and undulating astounded us. The profundity of it all. Around every curve an offering, swaths of intense yellow, flecks of crimson burning like love in the distant forests, and up high, slopes already naked, waiting for the weight and come of winter.

It seemed as if we needn't pedal at all and still we would ascend. Every mile higher and deeper the air grew tighter, colder. Mist danced in the dark trees and red leaves lay on the road like pieces from a puzzle.

Then, upon a great slow curve that moved around the side of a mountain like a vein, it was snowing. Just barely, bits of white scattering into the trees and bouncing down the road. I threw up my head and stuck out my tongue to catch one but they were too light and playful. I had been wanting snow. Snow is warmer than rain—doesn't seep into your bones. Snow will pop and skitter off your back and shoulders as if you were a bullet-proof man. But in a mile it stopped. Only teasing. The earth was too hot anyway, melting the little guys moments after they touched her.

The Urals are a long but narrow range and before lunch we reached the pass. There was a large stone pedestal off to the side and nothing else. The puddles in the gravel were plated with ice.

"All right?" shouted Torie.

"This is it!" shouted Tom.

Tanya squealed and rolled her eyes.

There was an aluminum pole stuck in the top of the pedestal. At the top of the pole, up in the snow now held fast in the sky, was a sign.

We could see our breath and our ears were numb and our noses were running off our faces. We were jogging in place and stomping our woolen feet and clapping our mittened hands.

When the Soviets arrived, we all climbed up on the pedestal together, tossed our arms in the frozen air, and screamed so the whole world would hear it. A truck driver snapped our picture.

Then we crawled down, pulled ourselves deeper inside our hoods and rode on. I looked back just as we were falling over the other side. The sign at the top of the pole was rigid in the slate sky.

There is one word on that sign.

SIBIR

We were in Europe now. We had bicycled across Siberia.

Two days later we split up.

It was a stone-cold evening, pouring black rain. It had been pouring black rain since noon the day before. Our clothes were frozen to our skin, our chins and lips so solid we slurred trying to talk.

"Tol'yatti!" Fyodor was bellowing insolently. The muscles under the fur on his face twitched.

"*Nyet*," said Tom calmly. He did not smile.

"TOL'YATTI!" Fyodor shouted again.

We were in the middle of the highway in the rain. Our bicycles lay in the mud in the barrow pit. We had stopped to camp. I'd splashed up and down in the fields on both sides of the road searching for a spot for the tents. There was none. The earth was under six inches of gray slush.

Tom and Fyodor were standing face to face.

"Fyodor," Tom spoke in Russian, the skin on his cheeks was

drawn, his eyes sagged, "look at Tanya. Look at Pavel. Look at me. We are cold and tired. We are shaking. You are shaking."

"*NYET*. Tol'yatti."

Tol'yatti was a city on the Volga River. It was sixty-five miles away.

"We should find a village."

"*NYET!*" Fyodor was shouting himself hoarse. His fists were clenched and he was quivering and the black rain was cutting him. I understood. Fyodor wanted to suffer. That is what he could do better than any of us.

"We should find a village." Tom's voice was an old man's, slow and very tired but very sure. "It will be dark in half an hour."

We'd ridden eighty-three miles and every mile had been agonizingly cold. The kind of cold that when you get off your bike you walk funny, bowlegged with your arms out because your fingers and toes ache so bad you're afraid they'll break off.

"*NYET!*" Fyodor puffed his chest at Tom.

Tom did not step back. His arms were down at his sides. Water was dripping off his nose and off the ends of his mittens.

"*Ya mushchina,*" Fyodor said wrathfully. I *man*. "I ride to Tol'yatti." He spewed it in Tom's face. I stepped up beside Tom.

"Yes Fyodor. You are a man," said Tom.

"*Koneshna, da!*" howled Fyodor.

"You should ride to Tol'yatti. We, however, will not."

"*Nu vy ZHENSHINY.*" You *WOMEN*.

Fyodor mounted and sprang off down the road. Pavel and Natasha both looked frightened, then grabbed their bikes and scurried after him.

That was the end of bicycling across Russia with Fyodor Konyukhov and Pavel Konyukhov and Natasha Traviynskay.

Tom dropped his head. He had wanted it to work so, so much.

"Hey, Thomas," I said, "good fucking riddance, OK."

It got him to grin.

It was raining hard and they were out of sight immediately. We pedaled to the first mud road and turned off.

We rode out through soaked fields to a village. On the edge of the village was a round babushka with a staff. Her staff was taller than she was. She was checking her garden. She lifted her head and watched us ride up to her. The mud was slick and deep and the tractor ruts threw us side to side. When we were close she pointed her staff down toward the log homes.

"Go to the club," she shouted. "It is cold. Go to the club."

In the village rain was skating off the metal roofs and the mud was too deep to ride. We pushed our bicycles. A woman came out to meet us. She was in green galoshes, carrying a bucket with a lid.

"Follow me," she said.

She was the schoolmaster. She said she had seen us coming through her window. She took us to the club.

"I will have the heat turned on," she said as she unlocked the padlock. "Now bring everything in."

We protested that we were covered with mud and she straightened her kerchief and pursed her lips.

"I can see that." She went to one of our bikes, picked it up with one hand and carried it herself up the wooden stairs. She turned on the lights, put the bicycle against the log wall and set the bucket on the table.

"Drink it," she said. "It is warm. Fresh milk." And she left.

We drank the milk and tried to dissect ourselves from our soaked clothes, but our fingers wouldn't work.

The clubhouse was painted green inside, log walls and plank flooring and a cardboard ceiling. At one end was a table, at the other end a tiny stage. The stage was so small I doubted that it could contain the breadth and contradictions and hope of even the simplest play. There were old red posters with powerful slogans on the walls. It was like a clubhouse or lodge in a Boy Scout camp generations ago, the kind of kinetic pubescent place where you learned patriotism and honor and destiny.

On one wall was a large painting of two men sitting across from each other. The painting was torn. It was Him and another fellow. They were dressed in tailored clothes and the scenery was unmuddy and manicured and they were drinking coffee from delicate china.

On the other walls were photos of old party leaders. They were dusty with those comical faces and long beards and sideways eyes that people always have in old photos.

The radiators started hissing. We each found one for ourselves and pressed against it and waited for the heat to uncripple us. When our fingers could move, we undressed and slowly laid our wet shirts and pants and underwear on our own radiators and stood there in sweaters and wool socks and wool hats and listened to the water sizzle.

We didn't talk much because it was too wonderful to talk.

We found a mop in the corner and tried to wipe up the mud puddles under our bicycles. We were coming back. We started to hop around, to skip and dance. We kidded and pinched and hugged each other the way you do in a clubhouse when you are very cold, inert cold, colder than being frozen and would give anything on earth, absolutely anything, just to be warm, and suddenly you are.

A knock came at the cabin door. Tanya ran over in her socks to open it and in stepped a man and a woman. They came inside only one step. The man was large and wore a suit and tie, derby hat and trench coat. He took off his hat and held it in his hands. The woman wore a plain skirt and also a trench coat. Both wore galoshes.

"Welcome to our village," the man said.

"You are so welcome," the woman said.

The man was the mayor of the village. This village was a dairy village. He was a member of the Communist party. He wore the pin on his lapel with pride. She was his wife.

"But what are you having for dinner?" the woman said. She had spotted the milk and half-loaf of bread on the table.

"And where are you going to sleep?" said the mayor.

Tanya tried to lie that we had plenty of food and unrolled her wet sleeping bag to show we had somewhere to sleep. They frowned and shook our hands and left.

Around eight that night we were just about to lie down when they came back. Once again they knocked, waited for us to open the door, and entered politely, as if their village clubhouse were our new home.

"Good evening again," said the mayor, hat in hand.

The mayor's wife had a cooked chicken in a pot and set it down on the table with pot holders and spun around and went back out. The mayor followed her. Then the schoolmaster who had guided us here came in carrying a large bowl of steaming potatoes. Behind her was the mayor with a great bundle of mattresses. He could barely get them through the doorway. His wife was right behind them with two loaves of hot bread wrapped in cloth. The mayor dumped the mattresses up on the stage and went back outside. Then the schoolmaster with a jar of homemade pickles and the mayor's wife with three liters of milk and the mayor with a load of quilts and feather pillows and the schoolmaster with two watermelons and the mayor's wife setting out plates and silverware and several jars of jam and honey and butter. We tried to protest and then tried to help but they would have none of it. When everything was arranged, the mayor spoke.

"Everyone asked why you do not come and spend the night in their home." Apparently he'd driven through the mud, house to house, collecting the mattresses and feather pillows.

"You could spend the night in any home in this village but you are in the old club." He looked around at the walls with the photos and banners.

"The club is never used now," his wife said. "You are the first to be here for a very long time."

"We are too wet and muddy for someone's home," said Tanya.

The mayor shook his head, his hat in his hands again.

"Pfff. *Balota*." He grinned. "*Balota* is everywhere. It means nothing. You could sleep in my bed."

The schoolmaster had disappeared. The mayor put his arm around his wife. They were standing together in the doorway. There was a feast on the table and mattresses and quilts and pillows on the stage and heat coming out so hot we had to take our clothes off the radiators, and the Soviets were somewhere outside in a stupor freezing horribly.

"*Spasiba, spasiba,*" over and over, was all we could say. They smiled and stepped out the door.

After we ate and were warm and dullheaded from the warmth and food and drunk with fatigue we shut off the lights and crawled together up on the stage. Heavy quilts were over us and great feather pillows surrounded us and the rain and mud were somewhere else and we were drifting and hearing each other breathing and no one spoke but Tanya.

Her voice was dreamy and soft as if she were already asleep.

"We could do this every night."

40

A ND WE COULD. Just the four of us, together. It was a raining Russian fall with iceblack nights and the earth tipped up and we streamed west and never camped again.

We could not ride through a village without being invited in. A night in a schoolhouse all wrapped around the coal furnace. A night with miners on their living-room floor. A night with a doctor who said she made 120 rubles a month and a night with a bus driver who said she made 300 and a night with farmers and one morning we rode into Moscow.

It had been 131 days since we were last in the Soviet capital. Torie and I pedaled slowly around St. Basil's. The sky was very gray. We pedaled around the Kremlin. The press and rumple-suits and the police and even Carl's film crew were all there asking questions but we couldn't speak, we couldn't answer. There was nothing left to say. We fled for the sanctuary of Russia.

Plunging and riding. A night with the union leader of a lumber mill taking the tour talking to the woman working the planers and a night in the physics lab of a high school and a night with an accountant and still plunging and riding *and there is the end. NO! the end flying up like a hummingbird zzz zzz in your face and dread big as a glass sliver coming out and it hurts because it has become a part of you and you don't want it to End. you want to keep going and going like a falling star in pitchblack but then just as*

249

much just exactly as much you want the whole fucking uncontrollable grandness of it all to end so bad you can't breathe about to faint lungs bursting you just want it to stop. stop. STOP!

And still riding. A night with a principal and with a waitress and we're never again eating in a *staloviya* but eating with Russians at their tables and never sleeping but sleeping in Russian beds toppling and tumbling and riding *riding forever just to get here only here and crossed right through the whole inconquerable sea to shining sea to say what it is you must say that is so so small.*

It had rained all day and it was still raining when we bicycled into a village and found three old ladies. They were on a bench below the eaves of a cabin. They were chatting sitting side by side and could have been sisters, all in wool.

It was fall and would turn to winter this night and they were warm and dry on their bench watching the storming as though it were a story.

We rode up and they looked at us. They weren't surprised because they were all babushkas and had seen everything there is to see.

The rain was sheeting off us and it was dark. The ladies waved us over and one stood up. She had her hands on her hips.

Shto vy delayiete pod dozhdyan, kogda moy dom tyoply?

What are you doing in the rain when my home is warm?

She pointed across the street to her cabin. She shook her head as if she were angry with us. As if she'd been on that bench all evening waiting for us and we were late. As if we'd sent a letter at the beginning from Nakhodka or a year ago from Wyoming or maybe our parents or grandparents had sent it, and the letter had made arrangements that we would be here this night at this time, and by all rights the letter should never have made it, but did.

Nu? Vy tol'ka stanyitye khalodnye.

Well? You're only getting colder.

She stepped out and the wind and rain hit her. She took us to her home.

There was a great broken white hearth in the middle of the cabin. She shoved wood in it and it pumped out heat. She picked up a yoke. She was going outside to carry water from the well. She would not let us help her.

We sat and listened to the storm. She brought in the pails and shook the water off her scarf. She made us sit next to the hearth while she fixed coffee. It was a special occasion and she used half of the tin she had hidden in her cupboard. Then she gave us burning soup.

When we were done she took the bowls from us, holding a kitten in her arms. She said she had four beds and that she had had four sons and they were all dead.

She lit a candle and took us in the back room behind the hearth. There was a picture of Jesus Christ on the wall.

On a shelf there was an ancient round Matrioshka doll. All the inside dolls had been taken out and carefully arranged together. They were each painted very differently. There were four of them.

She put us to bed and I could not fall asleep. I was in bed under quilts and warm in the dark and wondering what would happen *joy inside me like a kicking baby because we are finishing this journey but will never finish this journey never never never* and I could not fall asleep I could never fall asleep again and fell asleep.

I awoke because I heard scraping. I looked at my watch, it was four in the morning. I saw the babushka through a crack in the wall along the hearth. She was sitting on a stool with a knife, a bucket between her knees. She was peeling potatoes.

She had told us she would make potato soup for breakfast. I watched her peel potatoes in the dark and heard the scraping through the warm nightmorning.

Then she began to sing. She was a woman of great size but she sang softly. Softly.

41

On October 25, 1989, Tom Freisem, Torie Scott, Tanya Kirova and I bicycled into Leningrad. We rode to the Winter Palace. Through the arch with a bottle of champagne.

We rode in quietly under a low sky. We pedaled to the middle of the square across the cobblestones looking up at the palace. By now we knew we wouldn't feel what we thought we would feel.

We stood there straddling our bikes and somewhere far, far inside we wanted to howl crazy with glory and triumph, but we didn't. We felt like crying and shaking our fists in the air and then crawling off but we didn't do that either. We were tired. We were numb. We hugged each other and dumped the bottle of champagne over our heads and began to shiver because it was starting to snow.

Then we went to a hotel and slept for two days.

I got up once. I remember because I was dreaming something and it was very important but everything was happening to me again and I couldn't figure it out. I wasn't asleep or awake. I stood up and rummaged in the gear strewn through the room. Finally I found my journal. As I picked it up a letter fell out on the floor.

I sat down. It was a letter from Sue. The first letter.

Sitting on the floor in the dark holding the letter, I could feel her. I opened it and began to read and fell. Falling and swimming and falling. I saw her coming for me at last, and let go. Let go. I let go and began threading back upstream, stroking and falling and swimming, easily.

When I woke up Torie was pounding on the door.

"Mark. Mark. Are you ready for the end?"

We rode together out to the Baltic Sea and dipped our bikes in the ocean. Then we stood together in a huddle, Tom and Torie and Tanya and I, with our arms around each other and the cold blue water washing through our legs and we were already back home.

We heard the Soviets rode in one night but we never saw them.

Before we left Leningrad, once we realized what we had done, we had a party. We invited all our friends. Sasha from Krasnoyarsk and Sergei and Sasha from Chelyabinsk and Andrew from Omsk and all of *Western Siberia* and Saulius from Lithuania and many, many more.

And they all came. The airplane ticket cost each of them a month's salary and it was all for just one night and every last one of them came.

It was a party. Singing and drinking and dancing straight through to the morning. We sang hard and drank hard and danced hard as if it were our last night on earth. Because it was.

Sometime early, when it was snowing against the black windows and we were all humming a folk song soft as we could, I asked Saulius if he would come to my room.

We walked down the hall without speaking to each other. When we got to my door, I asked him to wait in the hall. I went inside and wheeled out Svabodny.

"This is for you."

Saulius did not move.

"It is too great a gift." His voice was almost inaudible. His hands were shaking.

"It is a very, very small gift."